LONGMAN LITERATURE

The Winslow Boy

Terence Rattigan

Editorial material: Jackie Head

Longman ▥

Contents

The writer on writing

Terence Rattigan was born in 1911 and died in 1977. He was one of the few British playwrights who succeeded in making a very comfortable living from his craft, having had nineteen plays produced in London between 1936 and 1977, all of which were enormously popular.

However, from his schooldays Rattigan had wanted to be taken seriously as a playwright, and that meant he had a desire for critical acclaim as well as popularity with audiences. He wrote in the 1953 preface to a compilation of his plays:

> Audiences, in short, are unreliable, wilful, incorrigible, obstinate, complacent, and hopelessly contradictory in their choice of entertainment.

Also in this piece he admits his obsession with what the critics had to say, as he recalls:

> reading over and over again, with wild anxious, red-rimmed, staring eyes, the brief paragraph.

Earlier plays by Rattigan

His first successful play, *French Without Tears*, produced in 1936, was well received by audiences and critics alike, but not expected to be the start of a line of hits. Being a young writer he was given credit for producing a *high-spirited charade*, a *youthful romp*, phrases which set the play down as amusing but ultimately unimportant. He was called *One-play-Rattigan* and complemented on this *lucky fluke*. One review, however, by James Agate of the *Sunday Times*, was particularly damning, dismissing the play as *Nothing. It has no wit, no plot, no characterisation, nothing.*

The play is set in a language school and Rattigan draws on his own experience of learning French and German at a 'crammer' during his summer holidays.

His next play, *Flarepath*, was written in 1942 after he had spent time serving in the air force. It is a play about the air force and was again popular with audiences. The critics continued to be lukewarm in their attitude towards his writing. Rattigan recalls: *I found myself commended, if not exactly as a professional playwright, at least as a promising apprentice who had definitely begun to learn the rudiments of his job.*

While the Sun Shines was his next play, produced in 1944. It maintained a focus on the military services and the attitudes and practices of middle-class England. Again the audiences flocked to see it, but the critics barely commented, implying, by their silence, that this form of 'light' comedy was not worthy of their interest. There was one exception. James Agate, who had been so scathing of his earlier work, wrote in the *Sunday Times* making a comparison between Rattigan and the respected playwrights Oscar Wilde and George Bernard Shaw and telling of Rattigan's *skill* and *craftmanship*. Although this did provide some acknowledgement of his talent, Rattigan did not consider it enough to call himself a success in terms of his own schoolboy aspirations. He saw the praise as limited, merely stating that he had, in his own words:

> a certain elementary sense of construction and a flair for the sort of glib and facile comic naturalism in which it appears that the actors are making up their own lines as they go along.

When *Love in Idleness* was produced in 1945 he chose Alfred Lunt, a well-known comic actor of the time, to take the main role and to direct the play. Lunt received high praise in the reviews following the production, which implied that it was he, not Rattigan, who had produced the comedy. Audiences enjoyed the play's run but the critics remained unexcited. Writing in 1945, Rattigan reflected on his role in the comedy, as the critics saw it:

> I was a wily compiler of stock comic situations and familiar comic characters, a fluent and by now experienced provider of opportunities for expert comedians to be expertly comic, and an unscrupulous exploiter of the notorious penchant of an English or American audience to laugh at almost anything provided they don't have to think.

The Winslow Boy

By the time Rattigan came to write his next play, *The Winslow Boy*, he was a commercial success and popular with audiences as a writer of 'light' comedies, but his worth as a writer was still largely unacknowledged.

The Winslow Boy is a very different play. Rattigan describes it as *serious comedy*, but one would also be forgiven for seeing it as not comic at all. It takes a weighty subject, the rights of the individual against the wishes of the state, and is set in the tense years of political unrest before the First World War. It debates the value of particular political parties, the position and rights of women and children in a male-dominated society, and, perhaps most importantly, it takes a real-life situation as the basis for the plot. Rattigan states that in its conception it was an idea-led play. In 1953, he wrote that the Archer-Shee case, on which the play is based, *had so fascinated and moved me that unlike many ideas that will peacefully wait in the store-room of the mind until their time for emergence has come, it demanded instant expression.*

Rattigan maintains that it was his interest in the case itself that shifted his emphasis from light to serious comedy. The plays which followed *The Winslow Boy* would seem to show this belief in the valid place of both types of drama, as he alternated between the two styles within them He wrote in 1945:

> *I never wavered in my own conviction that the three comedies had been critically misjudged; that, far from being aimless and vapid displays of juvenile high spirits, they were put together with the utmost care and craftmanship; that the absence of epigrams, literary phrasing, and verbal wit was deliberate and was not only not a vice but was in fact a virtue, representing on my part a notable triumph over the temptation of the adolescent to 'show off', finally that, despite the jeers of the serious-minded, the comedies had an element of pioneering and the experimental in them that had been entirely overlooked, and that did in fact allow me to claim to have contributed something, however small, to the development of the contemporary theatre.*

However, in one sense, he was conscious of the fact that writing a 'serious' play was more likely to bring him critical acclaim and not just the praise of audiences whom he saw could be *as attracted by the moronic as the sublime*. To some extent he saw his own popularity with audiences as a disadvantage in placing himself in the playwrights' 'hall of fame'. Many writers, whom the critics had praised and had since judged as part of the literary tradition, had written plays which had been received badly by audiences when first performed. So perhaps it was partly to give the critics what they asked for, a 'serious' play, that he took the line he did with *The Winslow Boy*.

When it was produced at the Lyric Theatre, London, in 1946, the critics did like the play. Rattigan says of their response:

It provided something of a critical sensation.

He found himself:

on the one hand warmly commended for my courage, and on the other sternly reprimanded for having hidden for so long my light under a bushel.

Although it wasn't referred to as a masterpiece it was seen as having a *sense of theatre*, to do with setting an audience thinking, not just with the business of craftsmanship or construction or language. Rattigan describes it thus:

Has not sense of theatre then something to do with the ability to thrill an audience by the mere power of suggestion, to move it by words unspoken, rather than spoken, to gain tears by a simple adverb repeated five times or in terms of comedy to arouse laughter by a glance or a nod? Surely, in comedy as in tragedy, it is the implicit rather than the explicit that gives life to a scene and, by demanding the collaboration of an audience, holds it, contented, flattered, alert and responsive.

Throughout the play this is clearly demonstrated by the number of questions left unanswered. It does not have a tidy, or even totally happy ending. Rattigan was asked to 'neaten' the ending before its first production and refused. The play presents us with problems and refuses to solve them, shows us different sides to an argument, but does not take sides, and makes Rattigan's own views, on the event and the results which follow, complicated and not completely clear. This uncertainly forms a large part of the play's appeal.

Introduction

The author and the play

Terence Rattigan was born in London in June 1911. His father was a British diplomat and spent most of his time abroad. Terence was born when the family visited England in 1911 for the coronation of George V, and they returned to North Africa soon afterwards. Much of Terence's young life was spent moving from one diplomatic posting to another, and being passed from the care of nannies to his grandmother in England, as his parents entered fully into the life of entertaining royalty and foreign ministers. When, during the early years of the First World War, his parents lived in France and Rumania he and his older brother Brian were separated from them for almost three years.

The relationship between his father and mother became strained at this time, and on their return the young Rattigan found himself taking sides with his mother against his father's unconventional behaviour in the Diplomatic Service and his adulterous relationships with other women. Terence was sent to Sandroyd, a prestigious preparatory school that led most of its pupils to Harrow, Eton or Winchester. His father had been educated at Harrow and it was expected that Terence would follow him there.

In 1922 his father resigned from the Diplomatic Service. Although not made poor as a result, the family no longer had the same comfortable means as previously, and had Terence not secured a scholarship he would not have been able to attend Harrow as planned. He began at Harrow in 1925, already determined to be a writer, and wrote a play *The Pure in Heart* at the age of fifteen. It was the story of a family who spent all their money sending their son to a public school, only to find that he wasted all his opportunities. This was an issue he returned to in the relative poverty brought upon the Winslow family in *The Winslow Boy*.

Although accepted as bright by the teachers, Rattigan was always a misfit with the pupils, despite his success in cricket, which would normally have led to popularity. He became interested in modern philosophers, Marx and Freud, and his liberal and humanist viewpoints set him at odds with his father and his Conservative friends. Terence objected to the school's compulsory Officers' Training Corps, and spoke against it, much to the annoyance of his father who had become a major in the First World War.

In 1930 he went up to Trinity College at Oxford, but spent his time playing sport, writing and acting in plays. He made friends amongst radicals who were labelled Communists for their debate on world pacifism which stated that this was more important than patriotism. Rattigan openly admitted that he had no intention of getting a degree. However, his father had hopes of him becoming a diplomat and sent him abroad during his holidays, to France for two years and Germany in his final year, in order to perfect his French and German. Whilst in Germany he wrote a play with a friend, at first called *Embryo* and later *First Episode*. It concerned the problems of loving relationships (an issue which he returned to in *The Winslow Boy* in Catherine's relationship with John Watherstone and Desmond Curry). It also explored his own uncertain feelings about homosexuality. This was the first of his plays to be staged, funded with money left to him by his grandmother, and written when he was twenty-two.

The Winslow Boy was produced in 1946, some thirteen years later. By this time Rattigan had already enjoyed great success with four previous plays, *French Without Tears*, which drew on some of his reactions to learning languages in the summer holidays, *Flarepath*, *While the Sun Shines* and *Love in Idleness* which gave a picture of the middle class in wartime. Now he was financially secure, he had fought in the Second World War (against his earlier pacifist convictions) and lost touch with many of his radical friends from college. His own political views were far less certain than they had previously seemed.

The period setting of *The Winslow Boy*

Throughout his life Rattigan was drawn to examine the period before the wars into which he was born. It was seen by the family as their heyday, being the time when his father enjoyed prestige and financial security in the Diplomatic

Service. For Rattigan it was a time of loneliness and separation from parental love. Britain was unsettled with its Liberal government which, though voted in on a wave of popularity in 1906, was then criticised for its emphasis on the needs of the state at the expense of the rights of the individual.

The trade unions were gaining power in the country: the seamen, railwaymen and dock workers all went on strike in 1911 to gain better pay and conditions. Also in that year the Insurance Bill was passed which imposed high levels of tax on the rich in order to fund sickness and unemployment benefits and pensions for the elderly. Women's suffrage (the fight for women to have the right to vote) was also an important issue, with public demonstrations by Emmeline Pankhurst and others who were sent to gaol for their forthright and 'unladylike' behaviour in trying to make their voices heard.

Perhaps prompted by new military strength in Europe, the country was building its own military and naval capacity and great importance was given to the powers of the Admiralty and other military institutions.

The Archer-Shee case

It was, therefore, surprising that against this background the government paid compensation of £3,000 to Colonel Archer-Shee for his son's expulsion from Osborne Naval College. It was alleged that the boy had stolen a five-shilling postal order, but the family, led by Archer-Shee's half-brother who was a Tory MP, fought against the dismissal. This action resulted in a public trial against the Admiralty, and was a clear indication of the tension between the Liberal government which represented growing state power, and public opinion amongst Tories and Liberals who felt that the rights of the individual were being forgotten.

Rattigan had always been interested in trials, and it was perhaps because of this, as well as a desire to bring to life his earliest years, that he chose to write *The Winslow Boy*.

The basic plot of the *The Winslow Boy* is taken from the Archer-Shee case. In previous plays Rattigan had invented his own plots, but here he had a very restricted canvas in which to tell the story. Rattigan said of the task, *I had therefore to fashion characters who could, because they actually did, only behave in a certain way.*

In many ways it is the characters as much as the plot which hold our interest. His approach to writing perhaps explains why this is: *I could only write my play by allowing my characters to make their own story.* Rattigan did take liberties with the details of the situation; he leaves out the half-brother from the play so that we are led to believe that the trial came about as a result of public pressure alone, rather than the persistence of politically motivated individuals. He makes Catherine, the older sister, a member of the suffragette movement when in real life she too was a Tory, and the father in the play is a retired bank manager, not a colonel as he was in real life.

The background to the play

Rattigan drew on many of the current events of 1911 to build the setting of the play.

The 1914-18 war

The forthcoming war gives a backcloth to the events which take place. It provides an argument for those who would stop the case continuing: *With the present troubles in the Balkans and a certain major European Power rapidly outbuilding our Navy, the Admiralty might be forgiven if it stated that it had rather more urgent affairs to deal with…*writes one of the appeal's opponents in *The Star* (Act 1, scene 2). The war is alluded to as Dickie joins the Territorials because… *from all accounts there is a fair chance of a bit of a scrap quite soon. If there is I don't want it to be all over before I can get in on it* – (Act 2, scene 2). Later in the same act we hear the news of John Watherstone: …*he thinks there's going to be a war. If there is his regiment will be among the first to go overseas.*

This looming war is looked forward to optimistically, and there is a strong sense of boredom with the present political scene and a belief that war is sport, soon won. Dickie, to some extent the voice of the average carefree young man, says, …*a chap can't help looking forward to a bit of a change – I can always go back to the bank afterwards* – (Act 2, scene 2).

Although the characters do not know what faces them, Rattigan did, as he was writing *after* two world wars. Many of his characters' words are laced with irony for the modern-day audience; we know for instance that the war will not be an end to dispute, and that, perhaps because of it, women will get the vote. But we do not know what will happen to these particular characters, and for this reason it is the people of the play, not the events, which provide our main focus.

The political scene and the growth of the trade unions

Rattigan makes passing references in the play to industrial unrest in the country, showing different attitudes towards this. When Catherine's father suggests Sir Robert Morton as advocate for the trial, she refers to his previous cases with disdain, saying he is popular because ... *if one happens to be a large monopoly attacking a trade union or a Tory paper libelling a Labour leader, he* is *the best,* and goes on to say, *I'm prejudiced because he's always speaking against what is right and just. Did you read his speech in the House on the Trades Disputes Bill?* (Act 1, scene 2). From this, and her earlier reading of the memoirs of Len Rogers, a trade-union leader, we know her interests are in supporting the unions, and as Catherine calls herself a radical and suffragette we can assume that these groups supported the increase in union power. We can also guess that her reactions throughout the play will to some extent be representative of these political groups.

In the same way we are persuaded at the start of the play that Sir Robert Morton represents the Tory view of the case. We can expect the rivalry that is seen when they first meet:

CATHERINE   *I was in court during your cross-examination of Len Rogers, in the Trades Union embezzlement case.*
SIR ROBERT   *Really?*
CATHERINE   *It was masterly.*
SIR ROBERT   *Thank you.*
CATHERINE   *I suppose you heard he committed suicide – a few months ago.*
SIR ROBERT   *Yes. I had heard.*
CATHERINE   *Many people believed him innocent, you know.*
SIR ROBERT   *So I understand.* (After a faint pause) *As it happens, however, he was guilty.*

(Act 1, scene 2, page 58)

At the end of the play it is these two rivals, brought closer together through the events of the trial and their own high sacrifices, who are left with the last word. This may suggest that the play does have a political message as much as a social one, or may just be an indication of Rattigan's own interest in these two characters of his creation, and his admiration for self-sacrifice.

The suffragettes

'The suffragettes' was the popular name given to the Women's Social and Political Union, the organisation formed in order to put pressure on the government to give women the right to vote in order to elect a government. By 1911 some steps had been made towards this with the right being given in 1907 for women to vote for, and be elected on to, parish councils. The presence of Miss Barnes in the play, as a lady journalist, does suggest a greater freedom for women, but she is not given any real power and is in many ways made ridiculous in her role as 'human interest' writer.

We learn most about the women's suffrage movement through the character of Catherine, who is organising secretary at the West London branch of the association. In her conversation with her mother in the first act we are given a hint of the movement's unacceptability:

GRACE   *Does John know you're a radical?*
CATHERINE *Oh, yes.*
GRACE   *And a suffragette?*
CATHERINE *Certainly.*
GRACE   (with a smile) *And he still wants to marry you?*

(Act 1, scene 1, page 8)

A later conversation between Catherine and Sir Robert (Act 2, scene 1) tells us that militants in the movement *go about breaking shop windows with a hammer* and *pouring acid down pillar boxes* and that Catherine, who is not a militant, works on a voluntary and unpaid basis. Later in the play when she asks for pay she is given two pounds a week; she acknowledges that this is all they can afford as they are *not a very rich organisation.*

Dickie's references to his sister's political beliefs express a gently mocking attitude – which was also present in pre-war Britain – towards the idea of women being given the vote:

DICKIE   *In your new feminine world do you suppose women will be allowed to do some of the paying?*

CATHERINE   *Certainly.*

DICKIE   *Really? Then the next time you're looking for someone to chain themselves to Mr Asquith, you can jolly well call on me...*

(Act 1, scene 2, pages 36-7)

Later in the scene he also voices a 'commonsense' view of the time: *Suppress your opinions. Men don't like 'em in their lady friends, even if they agree with 'em. And if they don't – it's fatal. Pretend to be half-witted, like Edwina, then he'll adore you.*

Rattigan does not make his own opinion clear on this or many of the other themes considered in the play. He is not represented by any single character, though many points of view are empowered with a certain dignity. One of these is certainly Catherine as she sacrifices her own comforts for the sake of her beliefs, which perhaps indicates a certain admiration for the suffragettes' cause. However, the figure of Miss Barnes also persuades us that he did not look on feminism without some doubt about whether it would work out in practice.

Conclusion

In looking at any play, we are always to some extent or other entering into the world of the playwright. In *The Winslow Boy* this is particularly so. When we look at these characters and settings we can see Rattigan exploring his own childhood and the sort of world into which he was born. We are given a picture of that world as he saw it, and through this we can begin to guess what Rattigan himself was like.

■ Reading log

One of the easiest ways of keeping track of your reading is to keep a log book. This can be any exercise book or folder that you have to hand, but make sure you reserve it exclusively for reflecting on your reading, both at home and in school.

As you read the play, stop from time to time and think back over what you have read.

- Is there anything that puzzles you? Note down some questions that you might want to research, discuss with your friends, or ask a teacher. Also note any quotations which strike you as important or memorable.

- Does your reading remind you of anything else you have read, heard or seen on TV or at the cinema? Jot down what it is and where the similarities lie.

- Have you had any experiences similar to those narrated in the play? Do you find yourself identifying closely with one or more of the characters? Record this as accurately as you can.

- Do you find yourself really liking, or really loathing, any of the characters? What is it about them that makes you feel so strongly? Make notes that you can add to.

- Can you picture the locations and settings? Draw maps, plans, diagrams, drawings, in fact any doodle that helps you make sense of these things.

- Now and again try to predict what will happen next in the play. Use what you already know of the author, the genre (type of story) and the characters to help you do this. Later record how close you were and whether you were surprised at the outcome.

- Write down any feelings that you have about the play. Your reading log should help you to make sense of your own ideas alongside those of the author.

The Winslow Boy

CHARACTERS
in the order of their appearance

RONNIE WINSLOW
VIOLET, *the Winslows' parlourmaid*
GRACE WINSLOW, *Ronnie's mother*
ARTHUR WINSLOW, *his father*
CATHERINE WINSLOW, *his sister*
DICKIE WINSLOW, *his elder brother*
JOHN WATHERSTONE, *engaged to Catherine*
DESMOND CURRY, *solicitor*
MISS BARNES, *journalist*
FRED, *Press photographer*
SIR ROBERT MORTON, *KC*

SYNOPSIS OF SCENES

The action of the play takes place in Arthur Winslow's house in Kensington, London, and extends over a period of two years preceding the War of 1914–1918.

ACT I
SCENE ONE – A Sunday morning in July.
SCENE TWO – An evening in April (9 months later)
ACT II
SCENE ONE – An evening in January (9 months later)
SCENE TWO – An afternoon in June (5 months later)

The play was inspired by the facts of a well-known case, but the characters attributed to the individuals represented are based on the author's imagination and not necessarily factual.

ACT I

SCENE I

The drawing-room of a house in Courtfield Gardens, South Kensington, at some period not long before the war of 1914-1918. It is a Sunday morning in July. The furnishings betoken solid but not undecorative upper middle-class comfort. On the table in the middle of the room are a cigarette box, a book and some periodicals. Two armchairs are near the fireplace and there are a number of upright chairs, one near the table. On a desk stand a telephone and a gramophone, both of pre-1914 vintage, the gramophone with a horn. A portrait of RONNIE *stands on the piano. One door leads to the hall, the other to the dining-room; french windows open on to the garden.*

Church bells are heard. As the curtain rises they fade. RONNIE, *a boy of about fourteen, is staring with wide, unblinking eyes at a portrait of himself on the piano. He is dressed in the uniform of an Osborne naval cadet. There is something rigid and tense in his attitude, and his face is blank and without expression. He turns and wanders aimlessly across to the fireplace. There is a sound from the hall. He looks despairingly round us though contemplating flight.* VIOLET, *an elderly maid, enters. At the sight of* RONNIE *she stops in the doorway in astonishment.*

VIOLET: Master Ronnie!

RONNIE (*with ill-managed sang-froid*): Hello, Violet.

VIOLET: Why, good gracious! We weren't expecting you back till Tuesday.

RONNIE: Yes, I know.

VIOLET: Why ever didn't you let us know you were coming, you silly boy? Your mother should have been at the station to meet you. The idea of a child like you

1

wandering all over London by yourself. I never did. How ever did you get in? By the garden, I suppose——

RONNIE: No. The front door. I rang and cook opened it.

VIOLET: Where's your trunk and your tuckbox?

RONNIE: Upstairs. The taximan carried them up——

VIOLET: Taximan? You took a taxi?

(RONNIE *nods.*)

All by yourself? Well, I don't know what little boys are coming to, I'm sure. What your father and mother will say, I don't know——

RONNIE: Where are they, Violet?

VIOLET: Church, of course.

RONNIE (*vacantly*): Oh, yes. It's Sunday, isn't it?

VIOLET: What's the matter with you? What have they been doing to you at Osborne?

RONNIE (*sharply*): What do you mean?

VIOLET: They seem to have made you a bit soft in the head, or something. Well—I suppose I'd better get your unpacking done—Mr. Dickie's been using your chest of drawers for all his dress clothes and things. I'll just clear 'em out and put 'em on his bed—that's what I'll do. He can find room for 'em somewhere else.

RONNIE: Shall I help you?

VIOLET (*scornfully*): I know *your* help. With *your* help I'll be at it all day. No, you just wait down here for your mother and father. They'll be back in a minute.

(RONNIE *nods and turns hopelessly away.* VIOLET *looks at his retreating back, puzzled.*)

Well?

RONNIE (*turning*): Yes?

2

VIOLET: Don't I get a kiss or are you too grown-up for that now?

RONNIE: Sorry, Violet. (*He goes up to her and is enveloped in her ample bosom.*)

VIOLET: That's better. My, what a big boy you're getting! (*She holds him at arm's length and inspects him.*) Quite the little naval officer, aren't you?

RONNIE (*smiling forlornly*): Yes. That's right.

VIOLET: Well, well, I must be getting on——

(VIOLET *releases him and goes into the hall.*)

(RONNIE *resumes his attitude of utter dejection. He takes out of his pocket a letter in a sealed envelope. After a second's hesitation, he opens it, and reads the contents. The perusal appears to increase his misery. He takes two or three quick steps towards the hall door. Then he stops, uncertainly. There is the sound of voices in the hall.* RONNIE, *with a strangled sob, runs to the window and into the garden.*)

The rest of the Winslow family enters from the hall.

ARTHUR WINSLOW, RONNIE'S *father, is about sixty with a rather deliberately cultured patriarchal air. He is leaning heavily on a stick.*

GRACE, *his wife, is about ten years younger and has the faded remnants of prettiness.*

CATHERINE, *their daughter, is approaching thirty and has an air of masculinity about her which is at odd variance with her mother's intense femininity. She carries a handbag.*

DICKIE, *their elder son, is an Oxford undergraduate, large, noisy and cheerful.*)

GRACE (*entering*): But he's so old, dear. From the back of

3

the church you really can't hear a word he says.

ARTHUR: He's a good man, Grace.

GRACE: But what's the use of being good, if you're inaudible?

CATHERINE: A problem in ethics for you, Father. (*She puts her handbag on the table, takes up a book, sits and reads.*)

(ARTHUR *looks round at the open french windows.*)

ARTHUR: There's a draught, Grace.

(GRACE *goes to the windows and closes them.*)

GRACE: Oh dear—it's coming on to rain.

DICKIE: I'm on Mother's side. The old boy's so doddery now he can hardly finish the course at all. I timed him to-day. It took him seventy-five seconds dead from a flying start to reach the pulpit, and then he needed the whip coming round the bend. I call that pretty bad going.

ARTHUR: I'm afraid I don't think that's very funny, Richard.

DICKIE: Oh, don't you, Father?

ARTHUR: Doddery though Mr. Jackson may seem now, I very much doubt if, when he was at Oxford, he failed in his pass mods.

DICKIE (*aggrieved*): Dash it, Father—you promised not to mention that again this vac——

GRACE: You did, you know, Arthur.

ARTHUR: There was a condition to my promise—if you remember—that Dickie should provide me with reasonable evidence of his intentions to work.

DICKIE: Well, haven't I, Father? Didn't I stay in all last night—a Saturday night—and work?

4

ARTHUR: You stayed in, Dickie. I would be the last to deny that.

GRACE: You *were* making rather a noise, dear, with that old gramophone of yours. I really can't believe you could have been doing much work with that going on all the time.

DICKIE: Funnily enough, Mother, it helps me to concentrate.

ARTHUR: Concentrate on what?

DICKIE: Work, of course.

ARTHUR: That wasn't exactly what you appeared to be concentrating on when I came down to fetch a book—sleep, may I say, having been rendered out of the question, by the hideous sounds emanating from this room.

DICKIE: Edwina and her brother just looked in on their way to the Grahams' dance—they only stayed a minute.

GRACE: What an idiotic girl that is! Oh, sorry, Dickie—I was forgetting. You're rather keen on her, aren't you?

ARTHUR: You would have had ample proof of that fact, Grace, if you had seen them in the attitude in which I found them last night.

DICKIE: We were practising the Bunny Hug.

GRACE: The what, dear?

DICKIE: The Bunny Hug. It's the new dance.

CATHERINE (*helpfully*): It's like the Turkey Trot—only more dignified.

GRACE: Oh, I thought that was the tango.

DICKIE: No. More like a Fox Trot, really. Something between a Boston Glide and a Kangaroo Hop.

5

ARTHUR: We appear to be straying from the point. Whatever animal was responsible for the posture I found you in has little to do with the fact that to my certain knowledge that you have not yet done one single stroke of work so far this vacation.

DICKIE: Oh. Well, I do work awfully fast, you know—once I get down to it.

ARTHUR: Indeed? That assumption can hardly be based on experience, I take it.

DICKIE: Dash it, Father! You are laying in to me, this morning.

ARTHUR: I think it's time you found out, Dickie, that I'm not spending two hundred pounds a year keeping you at Oxford, merely that you may make a lot of useless friends and learn to dance the Bunny Hop.

DICKIE: Hug, Father.

ARTHUR: The exact description of the obscenity is immaterial.

GRACE (*patting* DICKIE *on the head*): Father's quite right, you know, dear. You really have been going the pace a bit, this vac.

DICKIE: Yes, I know, Mother—but the season's nearly over now.

GRACE (*looking to the piano, at* RONNIE'S *portrait: with a sigh*): I wish you were as good about work as Ronnie.

DICKIE (*hotly*): I like that. That's a bit thick, I must say. All Ronnie ever has to do with his footling little homework is to add two and two, while I——

ARTHUR: Ronnie, may I remind you, is at least proving a good deal more successful in adding two and two than you were at his age.

DICKIE (*now furious*): Oh yes, I know. I know. He got into Osborne and I failed. That's going to be brought up again.

GRACE: Nobody's bringing it up, dear.

DICKIE: Oh yes they are. It's going to be brought up against me all my life. Ronnie's the good little boy, I'm the bad little boy. You've just stuck a couple of labels on us that nothing on earth is ever going to change.

GRACE: Don't be so absurd, dear——

DICKIE: It's not absurd. It's quite true. Isn't it, Kate?

(CATHERINE *looks up*.)

CATHERINE: I'm sorry, Dickie. I haven't been listening. Isn't what quite true?

DICKIE: That in the eyes of Mother and Father nothing that Ronnie does is ever wrong, and nothing that I do is ever right?

(CATHERINE *faces* DICKIE *for a moment before she speaks.*)

CATHERINE: If I were you, Dickie, dear, I'd go and have a nice lie down before lunch.

DICKIE (*after a pause*): Perhaps you're right. (*He goes towards the hall door.*)

ARTHUR: If you're going to your room, I suggest you take that object with you. (*He points to the gramophone on the desk.*)

(CATHERINE *returns to her book.*)

It's out of place in a drawing-room.

(DICKIE, *with an air of hauteur, crosses to the desk, picks up the gramophone and carries it to the door.*)

It might help you to concentrate on the work you're going to do this afternoon.

(DICKIE *stops at the door, and then turns slowly.*)

DICKIE (*with dignity*): That is out of the question, I'm afraid.

ARTHUR: Indeed? Why?

DICKIE: I have an engagement with Miss Gunn.

ARTHUR: On a Sunday afternoon? You're escorting her to the National Gallery, no doubt?

DICKIE: No. The Victoria and Albert Museum.

(DICKIE *goes out with as much dignity as is consistent with the carrying of a very bulky gramophone.* ARTHUR *picks up "Punch" from the table and sits in his chair.*)

GRACE: How stupid of him to say that about labels. (*She turns to the window*) There's no truth in it at all—is there, Kate?

CATHERINE (*deep in her book*): No, Mother.

GRACE: Oh dear, it's simply pelting. What are you reading, Kate?

CATHERINE: Len Rogers' Memoirs.

GRACE: Who's Len Rogers?

CATHERINE: A Trades Union Leader.

GRACE: Does John know you're a radical.

CATHERINE: Oh, yes.

GRACE: And a suffragette?

CATHERINE: Certainly.

GRACE (*with a smile*): And he still wants to marry you?

CATHERINE: He seems to.

GRACE: Oh, by the way, I've told him to come early for lunch—so that he can have a few words with Father first.

CATHERINE: Good idea. (*To* ARTHUR) I hope you've been primed, have you, Father? (*She rises and goes to* ARTHUR.)

ARTHUR: What's that?

CATHERINE (*sitting on the arm of* ARTHUR'S *chair*): You know what you're going to say to John, don't you? You're not going to let me down and forbid the match, or anything, are you? Because I warn you, if you do, I shall elope.

ARTHUR (*taking her hand*): Never fear, my dear. I'm far too delighted at the prospect of getting you off our hands at last.

CATHERINE (*smiling*): I'm not sure I like that "at last".

GRACE: Do you love him, dear?

CATHERINE: John? Yes, I do.

GRACE: You're such a funny girl. You never show your feelings much, do you? You don't behave as if you were in love.

CATHERINE: How does one behave as if one is in love?

ARTHUR: One doesn't read Len Rogers. One reads Byron.

CATHERINE: I do both.

ARTHUR: An odd combination.

CATHERINE: A satisfying one.

GRACE: I meant—you don't talk about him much, do you?

CATHERINE: No. I suppose I don't.

9

GRACE (*sighing*): I don't think you modern girls have the feelings our generation did. It's this New Woman attitude.

CATHERINE (*rising and facing* GRACE): Very well, Mother. I love John in every way that a woman can love a man, and far, far more than he loves me. Does that satisfy you?

GRACE (*embarrassed*): Well, really, Kate darling—I didn't ask for anything quite like that——(To ARTHUR) What are you laughing at, Arthur?

ARTHUR (*chuckling*): One up to the New Woman.

GRACE: Nonsense. (*She turns and goes towards the window*) She misunderstood me that's all. Just look at the rain! (*She turns to* CATHERINE) Kate, darling, does Desmond know about you and John?

CATHERINE: I haven't told him. On the other hand, if he hasn't guessed, he must be very dense.

ARTHUR: He *is* very dense.

GRACE: Oh, no. He's quite clever, if you really get under his skin.

ARTHUR: Oddly enough, I've never had that inclination.

(CATHERINE *smiles.*)

GRACE: I think he's a dear. Kate, darling, you will be kind to him, won't you?

CATHERINE (*patiently*): Yes, Mother. Of course I will.

GRACE: Poor Desmond! He's really a very good sort—— (*She breaks off suddenly and stares out of the window*) Hullo! There's someone in our garden.

CATHERINE (*going to the window*): Where?

GRACE (*pointing*): Over there, do you see?

CATHERINE: No.

GRACE: He's just gone behind that bush. It was a boy, I think. Probably Mrs. Williamson's awful little Dennis.

CATHERINE: Well, whoever it is must be getting terribly wet.

GRACE: Why can't he stick to his own garden?
  (*There is a sound of voices outside in the hall.*)
Is that John?

CATHERINE: It sounded like it.

  (*They both listen for a moment.*)

GRACE: Yes. It's John. (*To* CATHERINE) Quick! In the dining-room!

CATHERINE: All right. (*She dashes across to the dining-room door.*)

GRACE: Here! You've forgotten your bag. (*She darts to the table, picks up the bag and takes it to* CATHERINE.)

  (CATHERINE *takes the bag and goes out into the dining-room.*)

ARTHUR (*startled*): What on earth is going on?

GRACE (*In a stage whisper*): We're leaving you alone with John. When you've finished, cough or something.

ARTHUR (*testily*): What do you mean, or something?

GRACE: I know. Knock on the floor with your stick—three times. Then we'll come in.

ARTHUR: You don't think that might look a trifle co-incidental?

GRACE: Sh!
  (GRACE *disappears into the dining-room. At the same moment* VIOLET *enters from the hall.*)

VIOLET (*announcing*): Mr. Watherstone.

(JOHN WATHERSTONE *comes in. He is a man of about thirty, dressed in an extremely well-cut morning coat and striped trousers, an attire which, though excused by church parade, we may well feel has been donned for this occasion.* VIOLET *goes out.*)

ARTHUR: How are you, John? I'm very glad to see you.

JOHN: How do you do, sir?

ARTHUR: Will you forgive me not getting up? My arthritis has been troubling me rather a lot, lately.

JOHN: I'm very sorry to hear that, sir. Catherine told me it was better.

ARTHUR: It was, for a time. Now it's worse again. Do you smoke? (*He indicates the cigarette box on the table.*)

JOHN: Yes, sir. I do. Thank you. (*He takes a cigarette, and adds hastily*) In moderation, of course.

ARTHUR (*with a faint smile*): Of course.

(*Pause, while* JOHN *lights his cigarette.* ARTHUR *watches him.*)

Well, now, I understand you wish to marry my daughter.

JOHN: Yes, sir. That's to say, I've proposed to her and she's done me the honour of accepting me.

ARTHUR: I see. I trust when you corrected yourself, your second statement wasn't a denial of your first?
(JOHN *looks puzzled.*)
I mean, you do *really* wish to marry her?

JOHN: Of course, sir.

ARTHUR: Why of course? There are plenty of people about who don't wish to marry her.

JOHN: I meant, of course, because I proposed to her.

12

ARTHUR: That, too, doesn't necessarily follow. However, we don't need to quibble. We'll take the sentimental side of the project for granted. As regards the more practical aspect, perhaps you won't mind if I ask you a few rather personal questions. (*He waves* JOHN *to a chair*.)

JOHN (*sitting*): Naturally not, sir. It's your duty.

ARTHUR: Quite so. Now your income: are you able to live on it?

JOHN: No, sir. I'm in the regular army.

ARTHUR: Yes, of course.

JOHN: But my army pay is supplemented by an allowance from my father.

ARTHUR: So I understand. Now your father's would be, I take it, about twenty-four pounds a month.

JOHN (*surprised*): Yes, sir, that's exactly right.

ARTHUR: So that your total income—with your subaltern's pay and allowances plus the allowance from your father, would be, I take it, about four hundred and twenty pounds a year.

JOHN (*more surprised*): Again, exactly the figure.

ARTHUR: Well, well. It all seems perfectly satisfactory. I really don't think I need delay my congratulations any longer.

(ARTHUR *extends his hand.* JOHN *rises and takes it
gratefully*.)

JOHN: Thank you, sir, very much.

ARTHUR: I must say, it was very good of you to be so frank and informative.

JOHN: Not at all.

ARTHUR: Your answers to my questions deserve an equal frankness from me about Catherine's own affairs. I'm afraid she's not—just in case you thought otherwise—the daughter of a rich man.

JOHN: I didn't think otherwise, sir.

ARTHUR: Good. Well, now—— (*He suddenly cocks his head on one side and listens. There is the sound of a gramophone playing "Hitchey-Koo" from somewhere upstairs.*)
Would you be so good as to touch the bell?
(JOHN *crosses to the fireplace and rings the bell. It is heard distantly.*)
Thank you. Well, now, continuing about my own financial affairs. The Westminster Bank pay me a small pension —three hundred and fifty to be precise—and my wife has about two hundred a year of her own. Apart from that we have nothing, except such savings as I've been able to make during my career at the bank—the interest from which raises my total income to about eight hundred pounds per annum.

(VIOLET *comes in.*)

VIOLET: You rang, sir?

ARTHUR: Yes, Violet, my compliments to Mr. Dickie and if he doesn't stop that cacophonous hullabaloo at once, I'll throw him and his infernal machine into the street.

VIOLET: Yes, sir. What was that word again? Cac-some-thing——

ARTHUR: Never mind. Say anything you like, only stop him.

VIOLET: Well, sir, I'll do my best, but you know what Master Dickie's like with his blessed old ragtime.

ARTHUR: Yes, Violet, I do.

VIOLET: I could say you don't think it's quite nice on a Sunday.

ARTHUR (*roaring*): You can say I don't think it's quite nice on any day. Just stop him making that confounded din, that's all.

VIOLET: Yes, sir.

(VIOLET *goes out.*)

ARTHUR (*apologetically*): Our Violet has no doubt already been explained to you?

JOHN: I don't think so. Is any explanation necessary?

ARTHUR: I fear it is. She came to us direct from an orphanage a very long time ago, as a sort of under-between maid on probation, and in that capacity she was quite satisfactory; but I'm afraid, as parlourmaid, she has developed certain marked eccentricities in the performance of her duties—due, no doubt, to the fact that she has never fully known what they were. Well, now, where were we? Ah yes. I was telling you about my sources of income, was I not?

JOHN: Yes, sir.

ARTHUR: Now, in addition to the ordinary expenses of life, I have to maintain two sons—one at Osborne, and the other at Oxford—neither of whom, I'm afraid, will be in a position to support themselves for some time to come —one, because of his extreme youth and the other because of—er—other reasons.

(*The gramophone stops suddenly.*)

So, you see, I am not in a position to be very lavish as regards Catherine's dowry.

JOHN: No, sir, I quite see that.

ARTHUR: I propose to settle on her one sixth of my total capital—which worked out to the final fraction is exactly eight hundred and thirty-three pounds six and eightpence. But let us deal in round figures and say eight hundred and fifty pounds.

JOHN: I call that very generous, sir.

ARTHUR: Not as generous as I would have liked, I'm afraid. However—as my wife would say—beggars can't be choosers.

JOHN: Exactly, sir.

ARTHUR: Well, then, if you're agreeable to that arrangement, I don't think there's anything more we need discuss.

JOHN: No, sir.

ARTHUR: Splendid.

(There is a pause. ARTHUR takes his stick and raps it, with an air of studied unconcern, three times on the floor. They wait. Nothing happens.)

JOHN: Pretty rotten weather, isn't it?

ARTHUR: Yes. Vile. (He raps again. There is a pause. Again nothing happens.) Would you care for another cigarette?

JOHN: No, thank you, sir. I'm still smoking.

(ARTHUR takes up his stick to rap again, and then thinks better of it. He struggles out of his chair and goes slowly but firmly to the dining-room door. He throws open the door.)

ARTHUR (in apparent surprise): Well, imagine that! My wife and daughter are in here of all places. Come in, Grace. Come in, Catherine. John's here.

(GRACE comes in. CATHERINE follows.)

GRACE: Why, John—how nice!
(They shake hands.)

My, you do look a swell ! Doesn't he, Kate, darling?

CATHERINE: Quite one of the Knuts.

(*There is a pause.*)

GRACE (*unable to repress herself; coyly*): Well?

ARTHUR: Well, what?

GRACE: How did your little talk go?

ARTHUR (*testily*): I understood you weren't supposed to know we were having a little talk.

GRACE: Oh, you are infuriating ! Is everything all right, John?

(JOHN *nods, smiling.*)

Oh, I'm so glad. I really am.

JOHN: Thank you, Mrs. Winslow.

GRACE: May I kiss you? After all, I'm practically your mother now.

JOHN: Yes, of course.

(JOHN *allows himself to be kissed.*)

ARTHUR (*To* JOHN): While I, by the same token, am practically your father, but if you will forgive me——

JOHN (*smiling*): Certainly, sir.

ARTHUR: Grace, I think we might allow ourselves a little modest celebration at luncheon. Will you find me the key of the cellars?

(ARTHUR *turns and goes into the hall.*)

GRACE (*following him*): Yes, dear. (*She turns at the door; coyly*) I don't suppose you two will mind being left alone for a few minutes, will you?

(GRACE *follows her husband out.*)

CATHERINE: Was it an ordeal?

JOHN: I was scared to death.

CATHERINE: My poor darling——

(*She goes to him and they kiss.*)

JOHN: The annoying thing was that I had a whole lot of neatly turned phrases ready for him and he wouldn't let me use them.

CATHERINE: Such as?

JOHN: Oh—how proud and honoured I was by your acceptance of me, and how determined I was to make you a loyal and devoted husband—and to maintain you in the state to which you were accustomed—all that sort of thing. All very sincerely meant.

CATHERINE: Anything about loving me a little?

JOHN (*lightly*): That I thought we could take for granted. So did your father, incidentally.

CATHERINE: I see. (*She gazes at him*) Goodness, you do look smart!

JOHN: Not bad, is it?. Poole's.

CATHERINE: What about *your* father? How did he take it?

JOHN: All right.

CATHERINE: I bet he didn't.

JOHN: Oh, yes. He's been wanting me to get married for years. Getting worried about grandchildren, I suppose.

CATHERINE: He disapproves of me, doesn't he?

JOHN: Oh, no. Whatever makes you think that?

CATHERINE: He has a way of looking at me through his monocle that shrivels me up.

JOHN: He's just being a colonel, darling, that's all. All colonels look at you like that. Anyway, what about the way your father looks at me! Tell me, are all your family as scared of him as I am?

CATHERINE: Dickie is, of course; and Ronnie, though he doesn't need to be. Father worships him. I don't know about Mother being scared of him. Sometimes, perhaps. I'm not—ever.

JOHN: You're not scared of anything, are you?

CATHERINE: Oh yes. Heaps of things.

JOHN: Such as?

CATHERINE (with a smile): Oh . . . They're nearly all concerned with you.

(RONNIE looks cautiously in at the french windows. He now presents a very bedraggled and woe-begone appearance, with his uniform wringing wet, and his damp hair over his eyes.)

JOHN: You might be a little more explicit . . .

RONNIE (in a low voice): Kate!

(CATHERINE turns and sees him.)

CATHERINE (amazed): Ronnie! What on earth——

RONNIE: Where's Father?

CATHERINE: I'll go and tell him—— (She moves towards the door.)

RONNIE (urgently): No, don't; please, Kate, don't!

(CATHERINE stops, puzzled.)

CATHERINE: What's the trouble, Ronnie?
(RONNIE, trembling on the edge of tears, does not answer her. She goes to him.)
You're wet through. You'd better go and change.

RONNIE: No.

CATHERINE (gently): What's the trouble, darling? You can tell me.

(RONNIE *looks at* JOHN.)
You know John Watherstone, Ronnie. You met him last
holidays, don't you remember?
(RONNIE *remains silent, obviously reluctant to talk in front
of a comparative stranger.*)

JOHN (*tactfully*): I'll disappear.

CATHERINE (*pointing to the dining-room door*): In there,
do you mind?
(JOHN *goes out quietly.*)
Now, darling, tell me. What is it? Have you run away?
(RONNIE *shakes his head, evidently not trusting himself
to speak.*)
What is it, then?
(RONNIE *pulls out the letter from his pocket and slowly
hands it to her.* CATHERINE *reads it quietly.*)
Oh, God!

RONNIE: I didn't do it.
(CATHERINE *re-reads the letter in silence.*)
Kate, I didn't. Really, I didn't.

CATHERINE (*abstractedly*): No, darling. (*She seems uncertain of what to do*) This letter is addressed to Father.
Did you open it?

RONNIE: Yes.

CATHERINE: You shouldn't have done that——

RONNIE: I was going to tear it up. Then I heard you come
in from church and ran into the garden—I didn't know
what to do——

CATHERINE (*still distracted*): Did they send you up alone?

RONNIE: They sent a Petty Officer up with me. He was
supposed to wait and see Father, but I sent him away.
(*Indicating the letter*) Kate—shall we tear it up, now?

CATHERINE: No, darling.

20

RONNIE: We could tell Father term had ended two days sooner——

CATHERINE: No, darling.

RONNIE: I didn't do it, Kate, really I didn't——

(DICKIE *comes in from the hall. He does not seem surprised to see* RONNIE.)

DICKIE (*cheerfully*): Hullo, Ronnie, old lad. How's everything?

(RONNIE *turns away from him.*)

CATHERINE (*to* DICKIE): You knew he was here?

DICKIE: Oh yes. His trunks and things are all over our room. Trouble?

CATHERINE: Yes.

DICKIE: I'm sorry.

CATHERINE: You stay here with him. I'll find Mother.

DICKIE: All right.
(CATHERINE *goes into the hall. There is a pause.*)
What's up, old chap?

RONNIE: Nothing.

DICKIE: Come on—tell me.

RONNIE: It's all right.

DICKIE: Have you been sacked?
(RONNIE *nods.*)
Bad luck. What for?

RONNIE: I didn't do it.

DICKIE (*reassuringly*): No, of course you didn't.

RONNIE: Honestly, I didn't.

DICKIE: That's all right, old chap. No need to go on about it. I believe you.

RONNIE: You don't.

DICKIE: Well, I don't know what it is they've sacked you for, yet——

RONNIE (*in a low voice*): Stealing.

DICKIE (*evidently relieved*): Oh, is that all? Good Lord! I didn't know they sacked chaps for *that*, these days.

RONNIE: I didn't do it.

DICKIE: Why, good heavens, at school we used to pinch everything we could jolly well lay our hands on. All of us. (*As he speaks he quietly approaches* RONNIE) I remember there was one chap—Carstairs his name was—captain of cricket, believe it or not—absolutely nothing was safe with him—nothing at all. Pinched a squash racket of mine once, I remember—— (*He puts his arm on* RONNIE'S *shoulder*) Believe me, old chap, pinching's nothing. Nothing at all. I say—you're a bit damp, aren't you?

RONNIE: I've been out in the rain.

DICKIE: You're shivering a bit, too, aren't you? Oughtn't you to go and change? I mean, we don't want you catching pneumonia——

RONNIE: I'm all right.

(GRACE *comes in with* CATHERINE. GRACE *comes quickly to* RONNIE. *He sees her, turns away from* DICKIE *and runs into her arms.*)

GRACE: There, darling! It's all right, now.

(RONNIE *begins to cry quietly, his head buried in her dress.*)

RONNIE (*his voice muffled*): I didn't do it, Mother.

GRACE: No, darling. Of course you didn't. We'll go upstairs now, shall we, and get out of these nasty wet clothes?

RONNIE: Don't tell Father.

GRACE: No, darling. Not yet. I promise. Come along, now.
(*She leads him towards the hall door.*)
Your new uniform, too. What a shame!

(GRACE *and* RONNIE *go out.*)

DICKIE: I'd better go and keep *cave* for them. Ward off the
old man if he looks like going upstairs.
(CATHERINE *nods.*)
I say—who's going to break the news to him eventually?
I mean, someone'll have to.

CATHERINE: Don't let's worry about that now.

DICKIE: Well, you can count me out. In fact I don't want
to be within a thousand miles of that explosion.

(DICKIE *goes into the hall.* CATHERINE *opens the
dining-room door.*)

CATHERINE (*calling*): John.

JOHN (*entering*): Bad news?
(CATHERINE *nods.*)
That's rotten for you. I'm awfully sorry.

CATHERINE (*violently*): How can people be so cruel?

JOHN (*uncomfortably*): Expelled, I suppose?

(JOHN *gets his answer from* CATHERINE'S *silence, while she
recovers herself.*)

CATHERINE: God, how little imagination some people have!
Why should they torture a child of that age, John?
What's the point of it?

JOHN: What's he supposed to have done?

CATHERINE: Stolen some money.

JOHN: Oh.

CATHERINE: Ten days ago, it said in the letter. Why on

earth didn't they let us know? Just think of what that poor little creature has been going through these last ten days down there, entirely alone, without anyone to look after him, knowing what he had to face at the end of it! And then, finally, they send him up to London with a Petty Officer. Is it any wonder he's nearly out of his mind?

JOHN: It does seem pretty heartless, I know——

CATHERINE: Heartless? It's cold, calculated inhumanity. God, how I'd love to have that Commanding Officer here for just two minutes. I'd—I'd——

JOHN (*gently*): Darling—it's quite natural you should feel angry about it, but you must remember, he's not really at school. He's in the Service.

CATHERINE: What difference does that make?

JOHN: Well, they have ways of doing things in the Service which may seem to an outsider horribly brutal, but at least they're always scrupulously fair. You can take it from me, that there must have been a very full enquiry before they'd take a step of this sort. What's more, if there's been a delay of ten days, it would only have been in order to give the boy a better chance to clear him-self——

(*He pauses.* CATHERINE *is silent.*)
I'm sorry, Catherine, darling. I'd have done better to keep my mouth shut.

CATHERINE: No. What you said was perfectly true——

JOHN: It was tactless of me to say it, though. I'm sorry.

CATHERINE (*lightly*): That's all right.

JOHN: Forgive me? (*He lays his arm on her shoulder.*)

CATHERINE: Nothing to forgive.

JOHN: Believe me, I'm awfully sorry. (*He pauses.*) How will your father take it?

CATHERINE (*simply*): It might kill him——
  (*There is the sound of voices in the hall.*)
  Oh, heavens! We've got Desmond to lunch. I'd for-
  gotten—

JOHN: Who?

CATHERINE: Desmond Curry, our family solicitor. Oh,
  Lord! (*In a hasty whisper*) Darling—be polite to him,
  won't you?

JOHN: Why? Am I usually so rude to your guests?

CATHERINE: No, but he doesn't know about us yet——

JOHN: Who does?

CATHERINE (*still in a whisper*): Yes, but he's been in love
  with me for years—it's a family joke——

  (VIOLET *comes in.*)

VIOLET (*announcing*): Mr. Curry.

(DESMOND CURRY *comes in. He is a man of about forty-five,
  with the figure of an athlete gone to seed. He has a
  mildly furtive manner, rather as if he had just absconded
  with his firm's petty cash, and hopes no one is going to
  be too angry about it.* JOHN, *when he sees him, cannot
  repress a faint smile at the thought of him loving*
  CATHERINE. VIOLET *goes out.*)

CATHERINE: Hullo, Desmond. (*They shake hands.*) I don't
  think you know John Watherstone——

DESMOND: No—but, of course, I've heard a lot about
  him——

JOHN: How do you do?

(JOHN *wipes the smile off his face, as he meets* CATHERINE'S
  glance. He and DESMOND *shake hands. There is a pause.*)

DESMOND: Well, well, well. I trust I'm not early.

CATHERINE: No. Dead on time, Desmond—as always.

25

DESMOND: Capital. Capital.

(*There is another pause.*)

JOHN ⎱ (*together*) Pretty ghastly this rain.
CATHERINE ⎰ Tell me, Desmond——

JOHN: I'm so sorry.

CATHERINE: It's quite all right. I was only going to ask how you did in your cricket match yesterday, Desmond.

DESMOND: Not too well, I'm afraid. My shoulder's still giving me trouble——
(*There is another pause*)
(*At length*) Well, well. I hear I'm to congratulate you both——

CATHERINE: Desmond—you know?

DESMOND: Violet told me, just now—in the hall. Yes—I must congratulate you both.

CATHERINE: Thank you so much, Desmond.

JOHN: Thank you.

DESMOND: Of course, it's quite expected, I know. Quite expected. Still, it was rather a surprise, hearing it like that—from Violet in the hall.

CATHERINE: We were going to tell you, Desmond dear. It was only official this morning, you know. In fact you're the first person to hear it.

DESMOND: Am I? Am I, indeed? Well, I'm sure you'll both be very happy.

CATHERINE ⎱ (*murmuring ⎰ Thank you, Desmond.
JOHN ⎰ together) ⎱ Thank you.

DESMOND: Only this morning? Fancy.

(GRACE *comes in.*)

GRACE: Hullo, Desmond dear.

DESMOND: Hullo, Mrs. Winslow.

GRACE (to CATHERINE): I've got him to bed——

CATHERINE: Good.

DESMOND: Nobody ill, I hope?

GRACE: No, no. Nothing wrong at all——

(ARTHUR *comes in. He carries a bottle under his arm and has a corkscrew.*)

ARTHUR: Grace, when did we last have the cellars seen to?

GRACE: I can't remember, dear.

ARTHUR: Well, they're in a shocking condition. Hullo, Desmond. How are you? You're not looking well.

DESMOND: Am I not? I've strained my shoulder, you know.

ARTHUR: Well, why do you play these ridiculous games of yours? Resign yourself to the onrush of middle age and abandon them, my dear Desmond. (*He rings the bell and prepares to draw the cork.*)

DESMOND: Oh, I could never do that. Not give up cricket. Not altogether.

JOHN (*making conversation*): Are you any relation of D. W. H. Curry who used to play for Middlesex?

DESMOND (*whose moment has come*): I am D. W. H. Curry.

GRACE: Didn't you know we had a great man in the room?

JOHN: Gosh! Curry of Curry's match?

DESMOND: That's right.

JOHN: Hat trick against the Players in—what year was it?

DESMOND: 1895. At Lord's. Twenty-six overs, nine maidens, thirty-seven runs, eight wickets.

JOHN: Gosh! Do you know you used to be a schoolboy hero of mine?

DESMOND: Did I? Did I, indeed?

JOHN: Yes. I had a signed photograph of you.

DESMOND: Yes, I used to sign a lot once, for schoolboys, I remember.

ARTHUR: Only for schoolboys, Desmond?

DESMOND: I fear so—yes. Girls took no interest in cricket in those days.

JOHN: Gosh! D. W. H. Curry—in person. Well, I'd never have thought it.

DESMOND (sadly): I know. Very few people would now-adays.

CATHERINE (quickly): Oh, John didn't mean that, Desmond.

DESMOND: I fear he did. (He pats his protuberant stomach) This is the main trouble. Too much office work and too little exercise, I fear.

ARTHUR: Nonsense. Too much exercise and too little office work.

(VIOLET comes in.)

VIOLET: You rang, sir?

ARTHUR: Yes, Violet. Bring some glasses, would you?

VIOLET: Very good, sir.

(VIOLET goes out.)

ARTHUR: I thought we'd try a little of the Madeira before luncheon—we're celebrating you know, Desmond——
(GRACE furtively indicates DESMOND.)
(He adds hastily)—my wife's fifty-fourth birthday.

GRACE: Arthur! Really!

CATHERINE: It's all right, Father, Desmond knows——

DESMOND: Yes, indeed. It's wonderful news, isn't it? I'll most gladly drink a toast to the—er—to the——

ARTHUR (*politely*): Happy pair, I think, is the phrase that is eluding you.

DESMOND: Well, as a matter of fact, I was looking for something new to say.

ARTHUR (*murmuring*): A forlorn quest, my dear Desmond.

GRACE (*protestingly*): Arthur, really! You mustn't be so rude.

ARTHUR: I meant, naturally, that no one—with the possible exception of Voltaire—could find anything new to say about an engaged couple——
(VIOLET *enters with a tray of glasses, followed by* DICKIE)
Ah, my dear Dickie—just in time for a glass of Madeira in celebration of Kate's engagement to John—— (*He begins to pour out the wine.*)

DICKIE: Oh, is that all finally spliced up now? Kate definitely being withdrawn to stud? Good egg!

ARTHUR: Quite so. I should have added just now—with the possible exception of Voltaire and Dickie Winslow. (*To* VIOLET) Take these round, will you, Violet?

(*There is a general buzz of conversation.* VIOLET *takes round the tray of glasses.*)

CATHERINE: Are we allowed to drink our own healths?

ARTHUR: I think it's permissible.

GRACE: No. It's bad luck.

JOHN: We defy augury. Don't we, Kate?

GRACE: You mustn't say that, John dear. I know. You can

drink each other's healths. That's all right.

ARTHUR: Are my wife's superstitious terrors finally allayed? Good. (*He takes a drink.*)

(*Toasting*) Catherine and John.

(*All drink*—CATHERINE *and* JOHN *to each other.* VIOLET *lingers, smiling.*)

(*seeing* VIOLET) Ah, Violet! We mustn't leave you out. You must join this toast.

VIOLET: Well—thank you, sir.

(ARTHUR *pours her out a glass.*)

Not too much, sir, please. Just a sip.

ARTHUR: Quite so. Your reluctance would be more convincing if I hadn't noticed you'd brought an extra glass——

VIOLET (*taking the glass from* ARTHUR): Oh, I didn't bring it for myself, sir. I brought it for Master Ronnie—— (*She extends her glass*) Miss Kate and Mr. John. (*She takes a sip.*)

ARTHUR: You brought an extra glass for Master Ronnie, Violet?

VIOLET (*mistaking his bewilderment*): Well—I thought you might allow him just a sip, sir. Just to drink the toast. He's that grown-up these days.

(DESMOND *is staring gloomily into his glass. The others are frozen with apprehension.*)

ARTHUR: Master Ronnie isn't due back from Osborne until Tuesday, Violet.

VIOLET: Oh no, sir. He's back already. Came back unexpectedly this morning, all by himself.

ARTHUR: No, Violet. That isn't true. Someone has been playing a joke.

VIOLET: Well, I saw him in here with my own two eyes,

sir, as large as life just before you came in from church
—and then I heard Mrs. Winslow talking to him in his
room——

ARTHUR: Grace—what does this mean?

CATHERINE (*instinctively taking charge*): All right, Violet.
You can go——

VIOLET: Yes, miss.

(VIOLET *goes out*.)

ARTHUR (*to* CATHERINE): Did you know Ronnie was back?

CATHERINE: Yes.

ARTHUR: And you, Dickie?

DICKIE: Yes, Father.

ARTHUR: Grace?

GRACE (*helplessly*): We thought it best you shouldn't know
—for the time being. Only for the time being, Arthur.

ARTHUR (*slowly*): Is the boy ill?
(*No one answers.* ARTHUR *looks from one face to another
in bewilderment.*)
Answer me, someone! Is the boy very ill? Why must I
be kept in the dark like this? Surely I have the right to
know. If he's ill I must be with him——

CATHERINE (*steadily*): No, Father. He's not ill.

(ARTHUR *suddenly realizes the truth from the tone of
her voice.*)

ARTHUR: Will someone tell me what has happened, please?

(GRACE *looks at* CATHERINE *with helpless enquiry.* CATHERINE
nods. GRACE *takes the letter from her dress.*)

GRACE (*timidly*): He brought this letter for you—Arthur.

ARTHUR: Read it to me, please——

GRACE : Arthur—not in front of——

ARTHUR : Read it to me, please.

(GRACE *again looks at* CATHERINE *for advice, and again receives a nod.* ARTHUR *is sitting with his head bowed.* GRACE *begins to read.*)

GRACE : "Confidential. I am commanded by My Lords Commissioners of the Admiralty to inform you that they have received a communication from the Commanding Officer of the Royal Naval College at Osborne, reporting the theft of a five shilling postal order at the College on the 7th instant, which was afterwards cashed at the post office. Investigation of the circumstances of the case leaves no other conclusion possible than that the postal order was taken by your son, Cadet Ronald Arthur Winslow. My Lords deeply regret that they must therefore request you to withdraw your son from the College." It's signed by someone—I can't quite read his name——

(*She turns away quickly to hide her tears.* CATHERINE *puts a comforting hand on her shoulder.* ARTHUR *has not changed his attitude. There is a pause. The gong sounds in the hall outside.*)

ARTHUR (*at length*) : Desmond—be so good as to call Violet.
(DESMOND *goes into the hall. The gong stops. He returns at once and* VIOLET *enters.*)
Violet, ask Master Ronnie to come down and see me.

GRACE (*rising*) : Arthur—he's in bed.

ARTHUR : You told me he wasn't ill.

GRACE : He's not at all well.

ARTHUR : Do as I say, Violet.

VIOLET : Very good, sir.

(VIOLET *goes out.*)

ARTHUR : Perhaps the rest of you would go in to luncheon? Grace, would you take them in?

GRACE (*hovering*): Arthur—don't you think——

ARTHUR (*ignoring her*): Dickie, will you decant that bottle of claret I brought up from the cellar?

DICKIE: Yes, Father.

ARTHUR: I put it on the sideboard in the dining-room.

DICKIE: Yes, Father.

(DICKIE *goes into the dining-room.*)

ARTHUR: Will you go in, Desmond? And John?

(DESMOND *and* JOHN *go into the dining-room.* CATHERINE *follows them to the door and waits.* GRACE *is still hovering.*)

GRACE: Arthur?

ARTHUR: Yes, Grace?

GRACE: Please don't—please don't—— (*She stops, uncertainly.*)

ARTHUR: What mustn't I do?

GRACE: Please don't forget he's only a child——

(ARTHUR *does not answer her.*)

CATHERINE: Come on, Mother.

(GRACE *goes up to* CATHERINE *at the door. She looks back at* ARTHUR. *He has still not altered his position and is ignoring her. She goes into the dining-room followed by* CATHERINE. ARTHUR *does not move after they are gone. After an appreciable pause there comes a timid knock on the hall door.*)

ARTHUR: Come in.
   (RONNIE *appears in the doorway. He is in a dressing-gown. He stands on the threshold.*)
Come in and shut the door.
         (RONNIE *closes the door behind him.*)

Come over here.
(RONNIE *walks slowly up to his father.* ARTHUR *gazes at him steadily for some time, without speaking.*)
(*At length*) Why aren't you in your uniform?

RONNIE (*murmuring*): It got wet.

ARTHUR: How did it get wet?

RONNIE: I was out in the garden in the rain.

ARTHUR: Why?

RONNIE (*reluctantly*): I was hiding.

ARTHUR: From me?

(RONNIE *nods.*)
Do you remember once, you promised me that if ever you were in trouble of any sort you would come to me first?

RONNIE: Yes, Father.

ARTHUR: Why didn't you come to me now? Why did you have to go and hide in the garden?

RONNIE: I don't know, Father.

ARTHUR: Are you so frightened of me?

(RONNIE *does not reply.* ARTHUR *gazes at him for a moment, then holds up the letter.*)
In this letter it says you stole a postal order.
(RONNIE *opens his mouth to speak. Arthur stops him.*)
Now I don't want you to say a word until you've heard what I've got to say. If you did it, you must tell me. I shan't be angry with you, Ronnie—provided you tell me the truth. But if you tell me a lie, I shall know it, because a lie between you and me can't be hidden. I shall know it, Ronnie—so remember that before you speak. (*He pauses.*) Did you steal this postal order?

RONNIE (*without hesitation*): No, Father. I didn't.

(ARTHUR *takes a step towards him.*)

ARTHUR (*staring into his eyes*): Did you steal this postal
order?

RONNIE: No, Father. I didn't.

(ARTHUR *continues to stare into his eyes for a second,
then relaxes.*)

ARTHUR: Go on back to bed.
(RONNIE *goes gratefully to the hall door.*)
And in future I trust that a son of mine will at least
show enough sense to come in out of the rain.

RONNIE: Yes, Father.

(RONNIE *goes out.* ARTHUR *crosses to the desk. He picks
up the telephone.*)

ARTHUR (*into the telephone*): Hullo. Are you there? (*He
speaks very distinctly.*) I want to put a trunk call
through, please. A trunk call . . . Yes . . . The Royal
Naval College, Osborne . . . That's right . . . Replace
receiver? Certainly. (*He replaces the receiver and then,
after a moment's meditation, turns and walks briskly into
the dining-room.*)

QUICK CURTAIN.

SCENE II

*The same, nine months later. It is about six o'clock, of a
spring evening.*

DICKIE *is winding up his gramophone which, somehow or
other, appears to have found its way back into the drawing-
room. A pile of books and an opened notebook on the desk
provide evidence of interrupted labours. He starts the
gramophone and it emits a scratchy and muffled rendering
of "Alexander's Ragtime Band." DICKIE listens for a few
seconds with evident appreciation, then essays a little pas
seul, at the same time reading the book. CATHERINE comes*

in. She is in evening dress. DICKIE *goes to the gramophone and stops it.*

DICKIE: Hullo? Do you think the old man can hear this upstairs?

CATHERINE: I shouldn't think so. I couldn't.

DICKIE: Soft needle and an old sweater down the horn. Is the doctor still with him? (*He changes the record.*)
(CATHERINE *nods.*)
What's the verdict, do you know?

CATHERINE: I heard him say Father needed a complete rest——

DICKIE: Don't we all?

CATHERINE (*indicating the books on the desk*): It doesn't look as if *you* did. He said he ought to go to the country and forget all his worries.

DICKIE: Fat chance there is of that, I'd say.

CATHERINE: I know.

DICKIE: I say, you look a treat. New dress?

CATHERINE: Is it likely? No, it's an old one I've had done up.

DICKIE: Where are you going to?

CATHERINE: Daly's. Dinner first—at the Cri'.

DICKIE: Nice. You wouldn't care to take me along with you, I suppose.

CATHERINE: You suppose quite correctly.

DICKIE: John wouldn't mind.

CATHERINE: I dare say not. I would.

DICKIE: I wish I had someone to take me out. In your new feminine world do you suppose women will be allowed to do some of the paying?

CATHERINE: Certainly.

DICKIE: Really? Then the next time you're looking for someone to chain themselves to Mr. Asquith, you can jolly well call on me . . .

CATHERINE (*laughing*): Edwina might take you out if you gave her the hint. She's very rich——

DICKIE: If I gave Edwina a hint of that sort I wouldn't see her this side of Doomsday.

CATHERINE: You sound a little bitter, Dickie dear.

DICKIE: Oh no. Not bitter. Just realistic.
(VIOLET *comes in with an evening paper on a salver.*)
Good egg! *The Star!*

(*They both make a grab for it and* CATHERINE *gets it.* DICKIE *cranes over her shoulder as she hastily turns the pages.*)

VIOLET: You won't throw it away, will you, miss? If there's anything in it again, Cook and I would like to read it, after you.

CATHERINE: No. That's all right, Violet.
(VIOLET *goes out.*)
Here it is.

"The Osborne Cadet." There are two more letters. (*Reading*) "Sir,—I am entirely in agreement with your correspondent, *Democrat*, concerning the scandalously high-handed treatment by the Admiralty of the case of the Osborne Cadet. The efforts of Mr. Arthur Winslow to secure a fair trial for his son have evidently been thwarted at every turn by a soulless oligarchy——"

DICKIE: Soulless oligarchy! That's rather good.

CATHERINE (*reading*): "It is high time private and peaceful citizens of this country awoke to the increasing encroachment of their ancient freedom by the new despotism of

Whitehall. The Englishman's home was once said to be his castle. It seems it is rapidly becoming his prison. Your obedient servant, *Libertatis Amator.*"

DICKIE: Good for old *Amator*!

CATHERINE: The other's from *Perplexed.* (*Reading*) "Dear Sir,—I cannot understand what all the fuss is about in the case of the Osborne Cadet. Surely we have more important matters to get ourselves worked up about than a fourteen-year-old boy and a five shilling postal order." Silly old fool!

DICKIE: How do you know he's old?

CATHERINE: Isn't it obvious? (*Reading*) "With the present troubles in the Balkans and a certain major European Power rapidly outbuilding our Navy, the Admiralty might be forgiven if it stated that it had rather more urgent affairs to deal with than Master Ronnie Winslow's little troubles. A further enquiry before the Judge Advocate of the Fleet has now fully confirmed the original findings that the boy was guilty. I sincerely trust that this will finally end this ridiculous and sordid little storm in a teacup. I am, Sir, etc., *Perplexed.*"

(*There is a pause.*)

DICKIE (*reading over her shoulder*): "This correspondence must now cease.—Editor." Damn!

CATHERINE: Oh dear! (*She sits in the chair.*) How hopeless it seems sometimes.

DICKIE: Yes, it does, doesn't it? (*He pauses. Thoughtfully*): You know, Kate—don't give me away to the old man, will you?—but the awful thing is, if it hadn't been my own brother I think I might quite likely have seen *Perplexed's* point.

CATHERINE: Might you?

DICKIE: Well, I mean—looking at it from every angle and

all that—it does seem rather a much ado about damn all. I mean to say —a mere matter of pinching. (*Bitterly*) And it's all so beastly expensive . . . Let's cheer ourselves up with some music. (*He starts the gramophone.*)

CATHERINE (*listening to the record*): Is that what it's called?

DICKIE: Come and practise a few steps.
(CATHERINE *rises and joins* DICKIE. *They dance, in the manner of the period, with arms fully outstretched and working up and down, pump-handle style.*)
(*Surprised*) I say! Jolly good!

CATHERINE: Thank you, Dickie.

DICKIE: Who taught you? John, I suppose.

CATHERINE: No. I taught John, as it happens——

DICKIE: Feminism—even in love?
(CATHERINE *nods, smiling. They continue to dance.*)
(*After a pause*) When's the happy date now?

CATHERINE: Postponed again.

DICKIE: Oh, no! Why?

CATHERINE: His father's gone abroad for six months.

DICKIE: Why pay any attention to that old—— (*he substitutes the word*) gentleman?

CATHERINE: I wouldn't—but John does—so I have to.

(*Something in her tone makes* DICKIE *stop dancing and gaze at her seriously.*)

DICKIE: I say—nothing wrong, is there?
(CATHERINE *shakes her head, smiling, but not too emphatically.*)
I mean—you're not going to be left on the altar rails or anything, are you?

39

CATHERINE: Oh, no. I'll get him past the altar rails, if I have to drag him there.

DICKIE: Do you think you might have to?

CATHERINE: Quite frankly, yes.

DICKIE: Competition?

CATHERINE: Not yet. Only—differences of opinion.

(*They resume their dancing.*)

DICKIE: I see. Well, take some advice from an old hand, will you?

CATHERINE: Yes, Dickie.

DICKIE: Suppress your opinions. Men don't like 'em in their lady friends, even if they agree with 'em. And if they don't—it's fatal. Pretend to be half-witted, like Edwina, then he'll adore you.

CATHERINE: I know. I do, sometimes, and then I forget.

Still, you needn't worry. If there's ever a clash between what I believe and what I feel, there's not much doubt about which will win.

DICKIE: That's the girl! Of course, I don't know why you didn't fall in love with Ramsay MacDonald . . .

(ARTHUR *comes in. He is walking with more difficulty than when we last saw him.* DICKIE *and* CATHERINE *hastily stop dancing.* DICKIE *quickly turns off the gramophone.*)

CATHERINE (*quickly*): It was entirely my fault, Father. I enticed Dickie from his work to show me a few dance steps.

ARTHUR: Oh? I must admit I am surprised you succeeded.

DICKIE (*getting off the subject*): What did the doctor say, Father?

ARTHUR: He said, if I remember his exact words, that we

weren't quite as well as when we last saw each other. That information seems expensive at a guinea. (*He sees the evening paper.*) Oh, is that *The Star*? Let me see it, please.
(CATHERINE *gives him the paper.* DICKIE *sits at the desk and begins to read.*)
John will be calling for you here, I take it?

CATHERINE: Yes, Father.

ARTHUR: It might be better, perhaps, if you didn't ask him in. This room will shortly be a clutter of journalists, solicitors, barristers, and other impedimenta.

CATHERINE: Is Sir Robert Morton coming to see you here?

ARTHUR (*reading the paper*): I could hardly go and see him, could I?

(*There is a short pause.* DICKIE, *in deference to his father's presence, continues to work.* ARTHUR *reads* The Star. CATHERINE *glances at herself in the mirror, and then wanders to the hall door.*)

CATHERINE: I must go and do something about my hair.

DICKIE: What's the matter with your hair?

CATHERINE: Nothing, except I don't like it very much.

(CATHERINE *goes out.* DICKIE *opens two more books with a busy air.* ARTHUR *finishes reading the paper and stares moodily into space.*)

ARTHUR (*at length*): I wonder if I could sue *Perplexed*?

DICKIE: It might be a way of getting the case into court.

ARTHUR: On the other hand, he has not been libellous. Merely base. (*He throws the paper away and regards* DICKIE *thoughtfully.* DICKIE *is elaborately industrious.*)
(*At length, politely*) Do you mind if I disturb you for a moment?

DICKIE (*pushing his books away*): No, Father.

ARTHUR: I want to ask you a question, but before I do, I must impress on you the urgent necessity for an absolutely truthful answer.

DICKIE: Naturally.

ARTHUR: Naturally means by nature, and I'm afraid I have not yet noticed that it has invariably been your nature to answer my questions truthfully.

DICKIE: Oh. Well, I will this one, Father. I promise.

ARTHUR: Very well. (*He stares at him for a moment.*) What do you suppose one of your bookmaker friends would lay in the way of odds against your getting a degree?

(*There is a pause.*)

DICKIE: Oh. Well, let's think. Say—about evens.

ARTHUR: Hm. I rather doubt if at that price your friend would find many takers.

DICKIE: Well—perhaps seven to four against.

ARTHUR: I see. And what about the odds against your eventually becoming a civil servant?

DICKIE: Well—a bit steeper, I suppose.

ARTHUR: Exactly. Quite a bit steeper.

(*There is a pause.*)

DICKIE: You don't want to have a bet, do you?

ARTHUR: No, Dickie. I'm not a gambler. And that's exactly the trouble. Unhappily, I'm no longer in a position to gamble two hundred pounds a year on what you yourself admit is an outside chance.

DICKIE: Not an outside chance, Father. A good chance.

ARTHUR: Not good enough, Dickie, I'm afraid—with things as they are at the moment. Definitely not good enough. I fear my mind is finally made up.

(*There is a long pause.*)

DICKIE: You want me to leave Oxford—is that it?

ARTHUR: I'm afraid so, Dickie.

DICKIE: Oh. Straight away?

ARTHUR: No. You can finish your second year.

DICKIE: And what then?

ARTHUR: I can get you a job in the bank.

DICKIE (*quietly*): Oh, Lord!

ARTHUR (*after a pause: rather apologetically*): It'll be quite a good job, you know. Luckily, my influence in the bank still counts for something.

DICKIE: Father—if I promised you—I mean, *really* promised you—that from now on I'll work like a black——
        (ARTHUR *shakes his head slowly.*)
It's the case, I suppose?

ARTHUR: It's costing me a lot of money.

DICKIE: I know. It must be. Still, couldn't you—I mean, isn't there any way——
        (ARTHUR *again shakes his head.*)
Oh, Lord!

ARTHUR: I'm afraid this is rather a shock for you. I'm sorry.

DICKIE: What? No. No, it isn't really. I've been rather expecting it as a matter of fact—especially since I hear you are hoping to brief Sir Robert Morton. Still, I can't say but what it isn't a bit of a slap in the face——

(*The front door bell rings.*)

ARTHUR: There is a journalist coming to see me. Do you mind if we talk about this some other time?

DICKIE: No. Of course not, Father. (*He begins forlornly to gather his books.*)

ARTHUR (*with a half-smile*): I should leave those there, if I were you.

DICKIE: Yes. I will. Good idea. (*He goes to the door.*)

ARTHUR (*politely*): Tell me—how is your friend Miss Edwina Gunn these days?

DICKIE: Very well, thanks awfully.

ARTHUR: You don't suppose she'd mind if you took her to the theatre—or gave her a little present, perhaps?

DICKIE: Oh, I'm sure she wouldn't.

ARTHUR (*taking his sovereign purse from his waistcoat pocket. He extracts two sovereigns*): I'm afraid I can only make it a couple of sovereigns.

DICKIE (*taking them*): Thanks awfully, Father.

ARTHUR: With what's left over, you can always buy something for yourself.

DICKIE: Oh. Well, as a matter of fact, I don't suppose there will be an awful lot left over. Still, it's jolly decent of you. I say, Father—I think I could do with a little spot of something. Would you mind?

ARTHUR: Of course not. You'll find the decanter in the dining-room.

DICKIE: Thanks awfully. (*He moves towards the dining-room door.*)

ARTHUR: I must thank you, Dickie, for bearing what must have been a very unpleasant blow with some fortitude.

DICKIE (*uncomfortably*): Oh, rot, Father!

(DICKIE *goes out.* ARTHUR *sighs deeply.* VIOLET *comes in from the hall.*)

VIOLET (*announcing proudly*): The *Daily News*!

(MISS BARNES *comes in. She is a rather untidily-dressed woman of about forty, with a gushing manner.*)

MISS BARNES: Mr. Winslow? So good of you to see me.

ARTHUR: How do you do?

MISS BARNES (*simpering*): You're surprised to see a lady reporter? I know. Everyone is. And yet why not? What could be more natural?

ARTHUR: What, indeed? Pray sit down——

(MISS BARNES *sits.*)

MISS BARNES: My paper usually sends me out on stories which have a special appeal to women—stories with a little heart, you know, like this one—a father's fight for his little son's honour . . .

(ARTHUR *winces visibly.*)

ARTHUR: I venture to think this case has rather wider implications than that . . .

MISS BARNES: Oh yes. The political angle. I know. Very interesting, but not *quite* my line of country. Now what I'd really like to do is to get a nice picture of you and your little boy together. I've brought my assistant and camera. They're in the hall. Where is your little boy?

ARTHUR: My son is arriving from school in a few minutes. His mother has gone to the station to meet him.

MISS BARNES (*making a note*): From school? How interesting. So you got a school to take him? I mean, they didn't mind the unpleasantness?

ARTHUR: No.

MISS BARNES: And why is he coming back this time?

ARTHUR: He hasn't been expelled again, if that is what

you're implying. He is coming to London to be examined by Sir Robert Morton, whom we are hoping to brief——

MISS BARNES: Sir Robert Morton! (*She whistles apprecia-tively.*) Well!

ARTHUR: Exactly.

MISS BARNES (*doubtingly*): But do you *really* think he'll take a little case like this?

ARTHUR (*explosively*): It is not a little case, madam——

MISS BARNES: No, no. Of course not. But still—Sir Robert Morton!

ARTHUR: I understand that he is the best advocate in the country. He is certainly the most expensive——

MISS BARNES: Oh yes. I suppose if one is prepared to pay his fee one can get him for almost *any* case.

ARTHUR: Once more, madam—this is *not* almost any case——

MISS BARNES: No, no. Of course not. Well, now, perhaps you wouldn't mind giving me a few details. When did it all start?

ARTHUR: Nine months ago. The first I knew of the charge was when my son arrived home with a letter from the Admiralty informing me of his expulsion. I telephoned Osborne to protest, and was referred by them to the Lords of the Admiralty. My solicitors then took the matter up and demanded from the Admiralty the fullest possible enquiry. For weeks we were ignored, then met with a blank refusal, and only finally got reluctant permission to view the evidence.

MISS BARNES (*indifferently*): Really?

ARTHUR: My solicitors decided that the evidence was highly unsatisfactory, and fully justified the re-opening of proceedings. We applied to the Admiralty for a Court Martial. They ignored us. We applied for a civil trial. They ignored us again.

MISS BARNES : They ignored you?

ARTHUR : Yes. But after tremendous pressure had been brought to bear—letters to the papers, questions in the House, and other means open to private citizens of this country—the Admiralty eventually agreed to what they called an independent enquiry.

MISS BARNES (*vaguely*): Oh, good !

ARTHUR : It was not good, madam. At that independent enquiry, conducted by the Judge Advocate of the Fleet— against whom I am saying nothing, mind you—my son —a child of fourteen, was not represented by counsel, solicitors or friends. What do you think of that?

MISS BARNES : Fancy !

ARTHUR : You may well say "fancy."

MISS BARNES : And what happened at the enquiry?

ARTHUR : Inevitably he was found guilty again, and thus branded for the second time before the world as a thief and a forger——

MISS BARNES (*her attention wandering*): What a shame !

ARTHUR : I need hardly tell you, madam, that I am not prepared to let the matter rest there. I shall continue to fight this monstrous injustice with every weapon and every means at my disposal. Now it happens I have a plan . . .

MISS BARNES (*staring at the window*): Oh, what charming curtains ! (*She rises.*) What are they made of? (*She crosses to the window and examines the curtains.*)

(ARTHUR *sits for a moment in paralysed silence.*)

ARTHUR (*at length*): Madam—I fear I have no idea.

(There is the sound of voices in the hall.)

MISS BARNES *(brightly)*: Ah! Do I hear the poor little chap himself?

(RONNIE comes in, boisterously, followed by GRACE. He is evidently in the highest of spirits.)

RONNIE: Hullo, Father! *(He runs to ARTHUR.)*

ARTHUR: Hullo, Ronnie.

(GRACE greets MISS BARNES.)

RONNIE *(excitedly)*: I say, Father—Mr. Moore says I'm to tell you I needn't come back till Monday, if you like—so that gives me three whole days. *(He sits against the arm of the chair.)*

ARTHUR: Mind my leg!

RONNIE: Sorry, Father.

ARTHUR: How are you, my boy?

RONNIE: Oh, I'm absolutely tophole, Father. Mother says I've grown an inch . . .

MISS BARNES: Ah! Now that's exactly the way I'd like to take my picture. Would you hold it, Mr. Winslow? *(She goes to the hall door and calls.)* Fred! Come in now, will you?

RONNIE *(in a sibilant whisper)*: Who's she?

(FRED enters. He is a listless photographer, complete with apparatus.)

FRED *(gloomily)*: 'Afternoon, all.

MISS BARNES: That's the pose I suggest.

FRED: Yes. It'll do.

(He begins to set up his apparatus. ARTHUR, holding RONNIE close against him, turns to GRACE.)

ARTHUR: Grace, dear, this lady is from the *Daily News*. She is extremely interested in your curtains.

GRACE (*delighted*): Oh, really? How nice!

(*They move to the window.*)

MISS BARNES: Yes, indeed. I was wondering what they were made of.

GRACE

(*together*)

RONNIE

Well, it's an entirely new material, you know. I'm afraid I don't know what it's called, but I got them at Barker's last year. Apparently it's a sort of mixture of wild silk and . . .

Father, are we going to be in the *Daily News*?

ARTHUR: It appears so.

MISS BARNES

(*together*)

RONNIE

(*Now genuinely busy with her pencil and pad*) Just a second, Mrs. Winslow. I'm afraid my shorthand isn't very good. I must just get that down.

Oh, good! They get the *Daily News* in the school library, and everyone's bound to see it.

FRED: Quite still, please.

(*Everybody looks at* FRED. *He takes his photograph.*)
All right, Miss Barnes. (*He gathers up his apparatus and goes out.*)

MISS BARNES (*engrossed with* GRACE): Thank you, Fred. Good-bye, Mr. Winslow, and the very best of good fortune in your inspiring fight. (*She turns to* RONNIE) Good-bye, little chap. Remember—the darkest hour is just before the dawn. (*She turns to* GRACE) Well, it was very good of you to tell me all that, Mrs. Winslow. I'm sure our readers will be most interested.

RONNIE: What's she talking about?

(MISS BARNES *goes out with* GRACE.)

ARTHUR: The case, I imagine.

RONNIE: Oh, the case! Father, do you know the train had fourteen coaches?

ARTHUR: Did it indeed?

RONNIE: Yes. All corridor.

ARTHUR: Remarkable.

RONNIE: Of course, it was one of the very biggest expresses —I walked all the way down it from one end to the other.

ARTHUR: I had your half-term report, Ronnie.

RONNIE (*suddenly silenced by perturbation*): Oh, yes?

ARTHUR: On the whole it was pretty fair.

RONNIE: Oh, good.

ARTHUR: I'm glad you seem to be settling down so well— very glad indeed.

(GRACE *comes in.*)

GRACE: What a charming woman, Arthur!

ARTHUR: Charming. I trust you gave her full details about our curtains?

GRACE: Oh, yes. I told her everything.

ARTHUR (*wearily*): I'm so glad.

GRACE: I do think women reporters are a good idea.

RONNIE (*excitedly*): I say, Father—will it be all right for me to stay till Monday? I mean, I won't be missing any work—only Divinity—— (*He jogs his father's leg again.*)

ARTHUR: Mind my leg!

RONNIE: Oh, sorry, Father! Is it bad?

ARTHUR: Yes, it is. (*To* GRACE) Grace, take him upstairs and get him washed. Sir Robert will be here in a few minutes.

GRACE (*To* RONNIE): Come on, darling. (*She goes to the hall door.*)

RONNIE: All right. (*As he goes*) I say, do you know how long the train took? A hundred and twenty-three miles in two hours and fifty-two minutes. Violet! Violet! I'm back.

(RONNIE *goes out chattering shrilly.* GRACE *comes down to*
ARTHUR.)

GRACE: Did the doctor say anything, dear?

ARTHUR: A great deal—but very little to the purpose.

GRACE: Violet says he left an ointment for your back. Four massages a day. Is that right?

ARTHUR: Something of the kind.

GRACE: I think you'd better have one now, hadn't you, Arthur?

ARTHUR: No.

GRACE: But dear, you've got plenty of time before Sir Robert comes, and if you don't have one now you won't be able to have another before you go to bed.

ARTHUR: Precisely.

GRACE: But really, Arthur, it does seem awfully silly to spend all this money on doctors if you're not even going to do what they say——

ARTHUR (*impatiently*): All right, Grace. All right. All right. (*He rises.*)

GRACE: Thank you, dear.

(CATHERINE *comes in.*)

CATHERINE: Ronnie's back, judging by the noise——

GRACE (*examining* CATHERINE): I must say that old frock has come out very well. John'll never know it isn't brand new . . .

CATHERINE: He's late, curse him.

ARTHUR: Grace, go on up and attend to Ronnie and prepare the witches' brew for me. I'll come up when you're ready.

GRACE: Very well, dear. (*To* CATHERINE) Yes, that does look good. I must say Mme. Dupont's a treasure.

(GRACE *goes out.*)

ARTHUR (*wearily*): Oh, Kate, Kate! Are we both mad, you and I?

CATHERINE (*searching in her bag*): What's the matter, Father? (*She closes her bag and puts it down on the table.*)

ARTHUR: I don't know. I suddenly feel suicidally inclined. (*Bitterly*) A father's fight for his little boy's honour. Special appeal to all women. Photo inset of Mrs. Winslow's curtains. Is there any hope for the world?

CATHERINE (*smiling*): I think so, Father.

ARTHUR: Shall we drop the whole thing, Kate?

CATHERINE: I don't consider that a serious question, Father.

ARTHUR (*slowly*): You realize that if we go on, your marriage settlement must go?

CATHERINE (*lightly*): Oh yes. I gave that up for lost weeks ago.

ARTHUR: Things are all right between you and John, aren't they?

CATHERINE: Oh yes, Father, of course. Everything's perfect.

ARTHUR: I mean—it won't make any difference between you, will it?

CATHERINE: Good heavens, no!

ARTHUR: Very well, then. Let us pin our faith to Sir Robert Morton.
(CATHERINE *is silent.* ARTHUR *looks at her as if he had expected an answer, then nods.*)
I see I'm speaking only for myself in saying that.

CATHERINE (*lightly*): You know what I think of Sir Robert Morton, Father. Don't let's go into it again now. It's too late, anyway.

ARTHUR: It's not too late. He hasn't accepted the brief yet.

CATHERINE (*shortly*): Then I'm rather afraid I hope he never does. And that has nothing to do with my marriage settlement, either.

(*There is a pause.* ARTHUR *looks angry for a second, then subsides.*)

ARTHUR (*mildly*): I made enquiries about that fellow you suggested—I am told he is not nearly as good an advocate as Morton.

CATHERINE: He's not nearly so fashionable.

ARTHUR (*doubtfully*): I want the best——

CATHERINE: The best in this case certainly isn't Morton.

ARTHUR: Then why does everyone say he is?

CATHERINE (*roused*): Because if one happens to be a large monopoly attacking a trade union or a Tory paper libelling a Labour leader, he is the best. But it utterly defeats me how you or anyone else could expect a man of his record to have even a tenth of his heart in a case where the boot is entirely on the other foot.

ARTHUR: Well, I imagine if his heart isn't in it, he won't accept the brief.

CATHERINE: He might still. It depends what there is in it for him. Luckily there isn't much——

ARTHUR (*bitterly*): There is a fairly substantial cheque——

CATHERINE: He doesn't want money. He must be a very rich man.

ARTHUR: What does he want, then?

CATHERINE: Anything that advances his interests.

(ARTHUR *shrugs his shoulders.*)

ARTHUR (*after a pause*): I believe you are prejudiced because he spoke against women's suffrage.

CATHERINE: I am. I'm prejudiced because he is always speaking against what is right and just. Did you read his speech in the House on the Trades Disputes Bill?

GRACE (*off; calling*): Arthur! Arthur!

(*There is a pause.*)

ARTHUR (*smiling*): Oh, well—in the words of the Prime Minister let us wait and see! (*He moves towards the hall. At the door he turns back to* CATHERINE.) You're my only ally, Kate. Without you I believe I should have given up long ago.

CATHERINE: Rubbish.

ARTHUR: It's true. Still, you must sometimes allow me to make my own decisions. I have an instinct about Morton.
(CATHERINE *does not reply.*)

(*Doubtfully*) We'll see which is right—my instinct or your reason, eh?

(ARTHUR *goes out.*)

CATHERINE (*half to herself*): I'm afraid we will.

(DICKIE *enters from the dining-room.*)

DICKIE (*bitterly*): Hullo, Kate!

CATHERINE: Hullo, Dickie.
(DICKIE *crosses mournfully to the hall door.*)
What's the matter? Edwina jilted you or something?

DICKIE: Haven't you heard?
(CATHERINE *shakes her head.*)
I'm being scratched from the Oxford Stakes at the end of the year.

CATHERINE: Oh, Dickie! I'm awfully sorry.

DICKIE: Did you know it was in the wind?

CATHERINE: I knew there was a risk——

DICKIE: You might have warned a fellow. I fell plumb into the old man's trap. My gosh, I could just about murder that little brother of mine. (*Bitterly*) What's he have to go about pinching postal orders for? And why the hell does he have to get himself nabbed doing it? Silly little blighter!

(DICKIE *goes out gloomily. He leaves the door open. The front door bell rings.* CATHERINE *imagines it is* JOHN *and quickly picks up her bag, cloak, gloves and scarf and goes to the hall door.*)

CATHERINE (*calling*): All right, Violet. It's only Mr. Watherstone. I'll answer it.
(*She goes out. Voices are heard in the hall.* CATHERINE *enters with* DESMOND, *carrying a brief case, and* SIR ROBERT MORTON.)

SIR ROBERT *is a man in the early forties; tall, thin, cadaverous and immensely elegant. He wears a long overcoat and carries his hat. He looks rather a fop and his supercilious expression bears out this view.*)

(*As she enters*) I'm so sorry. I was expecting a friend.

(*She puts her possessions on a chair.*)

Won't you sit down, Sir Robert? My father won't be long.

(SIR ROBERT *bows slightly, and sits down on an upright chair, still in his overcoat.*)

Won't you sit here? (*She indicates* ARTHUR'S *chair.*) It's far more comfortable.

SIR ROBERT: No, thank you.

DESMOND (*fussing*): Sir Robert has a most important dinner engagement, so we came a little early.

CATHERINE: I see.

DESMOND: I'm afraid he can only spare us a very few minutes of his most valuable time this evening. Of course, it's a long way for him to come—so far from his chambers —and very good of him to do it, too, if I may say so . . . (*He bows to* SIR ROBERT.)

(SIR ROBERT *bows slightly back.*)

CATHERINE: I know. I can assure you we're very conscious of it.

(SIR ROBERT *gives her a quick look, and a faint smile.*)

DESMOND: Perhaps I had better advise your father of our presence——

CATHERINE: Yes, do, Desmond. You'll find him in his bed-room—having his leg rubbed.

DESMOND: Oh. I see.

(DESMOND *goes out. There is a pause.*)

56

CATHERINE: Is there anything I can get you, Sir Robert? A whisky and soda, or a brandy?

SIR ROBERT: No, thank you.

CATHERINE: Will you smoke?

SIR ROBERT: No, thank you.

CATHERINE (*holding up her cigarette*): I hope you don't mind me smoking?

SIR ROBERT: Why should I?

CATHERINE: Some people find it shocking.

SIR ROBERT (*indifferently*): A lady in her own home is surely entitled to behave as she wishes.

(*There is a pause.*)

CATHERINE: Won't you take your coat off, Sir Robert?

SIR ROBERT: No, thank you.

CATHERINE: You find it cold in here? I'm sorry.

SIR ROBERT: It's perfectly all right.

(*Conversation languishes again.* SIR ROBERT *looks at his watch.*)

CATHERINE: What time are you dining?

SIR ROBERT: Eight o'clock.

CATHERINE: Far from here?

SIR ROBERT: Devonshire House.

CATHERINE: Oh. Then, of course, you mustn't on **any** account be late.

SIR ROBERT: No.

(*There is another pause.*)

CATHERINE: I suppose you know the history of this case, do you, Sir Robert?

SIR ROBERT (*examining his nails*): I believe I have seen most of the relevant documents.

CATHERINE: Do you think we can bring the case into court by a collusive action?

SIR ROBERT: I really have no idea——

CATHERINE: Curry and Curry seem to think that might hold——

SIR ROBERT: Do they? They are a very reliable firm.

(CATHERINE *is on the verge of losing her temper.*)

CATHERINE (*after a pause*): I'm rather surprised that a case of this sort should interest you, Sir Robert.

SIR ROBERT: Are you?

CATHERINE: It seems such a very trivial affair, compared to most of your great forensic triumphs.

(SIR ROBERT *does not reply.*)
I was in court during your cross-examination of Len Rogers, in the Trades Union embezzlement case.

SIR ROBERT: Really?

CATHERINE: It was masterly.

SIR ROBERT: Thank you.

CATHERINE: I suppose you heard that he committed suicide —a few months ago.

SIR ROBERT: Yes. I had heard.

CATHERINE: Many people believed him innocent, you know.

SIR ROBERT: So I understand. (*After a faint pause*) As it happens, however, he was guilty.

(GRACE *comes in hastily.*)

GRACE: Sir Robert? My husband's so sorry to have kept you, but he's just coming.

(SIR ROBERT *rises. He and* GRACE *shake hands.*)

SIR ROBERT: It's perfectly all right. How do you do?

CATHERINE: Sir Robert is dining at Devonshire House, Mother.

GRACE: Oh, really? Oh, then you have to be punctual, of course, I do see that. It's the politeness of princes, isn't it?

SIR ROBERT: So they say.

GRACE: In this case, the other way round, of course. Ah, I think I hear my husband on the stairs. I hope Catherine entertained you all right?

SIR ROBERT (*with a faint bow to* CATHERINE): Very well, thank you.

(ARTHUR *comes in.* DESMOND *follows him.*)

ARTHUR: Sir Robert? I am Arthur Winslow.

SIR ROBERT: How do you do?

ARTHUR: I understand you are rather pressed for time.

GRACE: Yes. He's dining at Devonshire House.

ARTHUR: Are you, indeed? My son should be down in a minute. I expect you will wish to examine him.

SIR ROBERT (*indifferently*): Just a few questions. I fear that is all I will have time for this evening.

ARTHUR: I am rather sorry to hear that. He has made the journey especially from school for this interview and I was hoping that by the end of it I should know definitely yes or no if you would accept the brief.

DESMOND (*pacifically*): Well, perhaps Sir Robert would consent to finish his examination some other time? (*He opens his briefcase on the table and takes out some documents.*)

59

SIR ROBERT: It might be arranged.

ARTHUR: To-morrow?

SIR ROBERT: To-morrow is impossible. I am in court all the morning, and in the House of Commons for the rest of the day. (*Carelessly*) If a further examination should prove necessary it will have to be some time next week.

ARTHUR: I see. Will you forgive me if I sit down? (*He moves to his chair and sits.*) Curry has been telling me you think it might be possible to proceed by Petition of Right.

(SIR ROBERT *sits at the table.*)

CATHERINE: What's a Petition of Right?

DESMOND: Well—granting the assumption that the Admiralty, as the Crown, can do no wrong——

CATHERINE (*murmuring*): I thought that was exactly the assumption we refused to grant.

DESMOND: In law, I mean. Now a subject can sue the Crown, nevertheless, by Petition of Right, redress being granted as a matter of grace—and the custom is for the Attorney-General—on behalf of the King—to endorse the Petition, and allow the case to come to court. (*He moves the documents along the table in front of* SIR ROBERT.)

SIR ROBERT: It is interesting to note that the exact words he uses on such occasions are: Let Right be done.

ARTHUR: Let Right be done. I like that phrase, sir.

SIR ROBERT: It has a certain ring about it—has it not? (*Languidly*) Let Right be done.

(RONNIE *comes in. He is in an Eton suit, looking very spick and span.*)

ARTHUR: This is my son, Ronald. Ronnie, this is Sir Robert Morton.

RONNIE: How do you do, sir? (*He shakes hands with* SIR ROBERT.)

ARTHUR: He is going to ask you a few questions. You must answer them all truthfully—as you always have. (*He begins to struggle out of his chair.*) I expect you would like us to leave——

SIR ROBERT: No, provided, of course, that you don't interrupt. (*To* CATHERINE) Miss Winslow, will you sit down, please?

(CATHERINE *sits.*)

(*To* RONNIE) Will you stand at the table, facing me?

(RONNIE *does so.*)

That's right.

(*He faces* RONNIE *across the table and begins his examination very quietly.*) How old are you?

RONNIE: Fourteen and seven months.

SIR ROBERT: You were, then, thirteen and ten months old when you left Osborne; is that right?

RONNIE: Yes, sir.

SIR ROBERT: Now I would like you to cast your mind back to July 7th of last year. Will you tell me in your own words exactly what happened to you on that day?

RONNIE: All right. Well, it was a half-holiday, so we didn't have any work after dinner——

SIR ROBERT: Dinner?

RONNIE: Yes. At one o'clock. Until prep. at seven——

SIR ROBERT: Prep. at seven?

RONNIE: Yes. Just before dinner I went to the Chief Petty Officer and asked him to let me have fifteen and six out of what I had in the College Bank——

SIR ROBERT: Why did you do that?

61

RONNIE: I wanted to buy an air-pistol.

SIR ROBERT: Which cost fifteen and six?

RONNIE: Yes, sir.

SIR ROBERT: And how much money did you have in the College bank at the time?

RONNIE: Two pounds three shillings.

ARTHUR: So you see, sir, what incentive could there possibly be for him to steal five shillings?

SIR ROBERT (coldly): I must ask you to be good enough not to interrupt me, sir. (To RONNIE) After you had withdrawn the fifteen and six, what did you do?

RONNIE: I had dinner.

SIR ROBERT: Then what?

RONNIE: I went to the locker-room and put the fifteen and six in my locker.

SIR ROBERT: Yes. Then?

RONNIE: I went to get permission to go down to the post office. Then I went to the locker-room again, got out my money, and went down to the post office.

SIR ROBERT: I see. Go on.

RONNIE: I bought my postal order——

SIR ROBERT: For fifteen and six?

RONNIE: Yes. Then I went back to college. Then I met Elliot minor, and he said: "I say, isn't it rot? Someone's broken into my locker and pinched a postal order. I've reported it to the P.O."

SIR ROBERT: Those were Elliot minor's exact words?

RONNIE: He might have used another word for rot——

SIR ROBERT: I see. Continue——

RONNIE: Well then, just before prep., I was told to go along and see Commander Flower. The woman from the post office was there, and the Commander said: "Is this the boy?" and she said, "It might be. I can't be sure. They all look so much alike."

ARTHUR: You see? She couldn't identify him.

(SIR ROBERT *glares at* ARTHUR.)

SIR ROBERT (*to* RONNIE): Go on.

RONNIE: Then she said: "I only know that the boy who bought a postal order for fifteen and six was the same boy that cashed one for five shillings." So the Commander said: "Did you buy a postal order for fifteen and six?" And I said, "Yes," and then they made me write Elliot minor's name on an envelope, and compared it to the signature on the postal order—then they sent me to the sanatorium, and ten days later I was sacked—I mean—expelled.

SIR ROBERT: I see. (*He rises. Quietly*): Did you cash a postal order belonging to Elliot minor for five shillings?

RONNIE: No, sir.

SIR ROBERT: Did you break into his locker and steal it?

RONNIE: No, sir.

(DICKIE *enters. He stands furtively in the doorway, not knowing whether to come in or go out.*)

SIR ROBERT: And that is the truth, the whole truth, and nothing but the truth?

RONNIE: Yes, sir.

(ARTHUR *waves* DICKIE *impatiently to come and stand behind his chair.*)

SIR ROBERT: Right. When the Commander asked you to

write Elliot's name on an envelope, how did you write it?
With Christian name or initials?

RONNIE: I wrote: "Charles K. Elliot."

SIR ROBERT: Charles K. Elliot. Did you by any chance
happen to see the forged postal order in the Commander's
office?

RONNIE: Oh yes. The Commander showed it to me.

SIR ROBERT: Before or after you had written Elliot's name
on the envelope?

RONNIE: After.

SIR ROBERT: After. And did you happen to see how Elliot's
name was written on the postal order?

RONNIE: Yes, sir. The same.

SIR ROBERT: The same? Charles K. Elliot.

RONNIE: Yes, sir.

SIR ROBERT: When you wrote on the envelope—what
made you choose that particular form?

RONNIE: That was the way he usually signed his name.

SIR ROBERT: How did you know?

RONNIE: Well—he was a friend of mine——

SIR ROBERT: That is no answer. How did you know?

RONNIE: I'd seen him sign things.

SIR ROBERT: What things?

RONNIE: Oh—ordinary things.

SIR ROBERT: I repeat—what things?

RONNIE (reluctantly): Bits of paper.

SIR ROBERT: Bits of paper? And why did he sign his name on bits of paper?

RONNIE: I don't know.

SIR ROBERT: You do know. Why did he sign his name on bits of paper?

RONNIE: He was practising his signature.

SIR ROBERT: And you saw him?

RONNIE: Yes.

SIR ROBERT: Did he know you saw him?

RONNIE: Well—yes——

SIR ROBERT: In other words, he showed you exactly how he wrote his signature?

RONNIE: Yes. I suppose he did.

SIR ROBERT: Did you practise writing it yourself?

RONNIE: I might have done.

SIR ROBERT: What do you mean, you might have done? Did you, or did you not?

RONNIE: Yes.

ARTHUR (sharply): Ronnie! You never told me that.

RONNIE: It was only for a joke——

SIR ROBERT: Never mind whether it was for a joke or not. The fact is, you practised forging Elliot's signature.

RONNIE: It wasn't forging——

SIR ROBERT: What do you call it then?

RONNIE: Writing.

SIR ROBERT: Very well. Writing. Whoever stole the postal

order and cashed it also *wrote* Elliot's signature, didn't he?

RONNIE: Yes.

SIR ROBERT: And, oddly enough, in the exact form in which you had earlier been practising *writing* his signature.

RONNIE (*indignantly*): I say! Which side are you on?

SIR ROBERT (*snarling*): Don't be impertinent! (*He consults a document*) Are you aware that the Admiralty sent up the forged postal order to Mr. Ridgley-Pearce—the greatest handwriting expert in England?

RONNIE: Yes.

SIR ROBERT: And you know that Mr. Ridgley-Pearce affirmed that there was no doubt that the signature on the postal order and the signature you wrote on the envelope were by one and the same hand?

RONNIE: Yes.

SIR ROBERT: And you still say that you didn't forge that signature?

RONNIE: Yes, I do.

SIR ROBERT: In other words, Mr. Ridgley-Pearce doesn't know his job?

RONNIE: Well, he's wrong, anyway.

SIR ROBERT: When you went into the locker room after lunch, were you alone?

RONNIE: I don't remember.

SIR ROBERT: I think you do. Were you alone in the locker room?

RONNIE: Yes.

SIR ROBERT: And you knew which was Elliot's locker?

RONNIE: Yes, of course.

SIR ROBERT: Why did you go in there at all?

RONNIE: I've told you. To put my fifteen and six away.

SIR ROBERT: Why?

RONNIE: I thought it would be safer.

SIR ROBERT: Why safer than your pocket?

RONNIE: I don't know.

SIR ROBERT: You had it in your pocket at dinner-time. Why this sudden fear for its safety?

RONNIE (*plainly rattled*): I tell you I don't know——

SIR ROBERT: It was rather an odd thing to do, wasn't it? The money was perfectly safe in your pocket. Why did you suddenly feel yourself impelled to put it away in your locker?

RONNIE (*almost shouting*): I don't know.

SIR ROBERT: Was it because you knew you would be alone in the locker room at that time?

RONNIE: No.

SIR ROBERT: Where was Elliot's locker in relation to yours?

RONNIE: Next to it, but one.

SIR ROBERT: Next but one. What time did Elliot put his postal order in his locker?

RONNIE: I don't know. I didn't even know he had a postal order in his locker. I didn't know he had a postal order at all.

SIR ROBERT: Yet you say he was a great friend of yours——

RONNIE: He didn't tell me he had one.

SIR ROBERT: How very secretive of him. (*He makes a note on the document*) What time did you go to the locker room?

RONNIE: I don't remember.

SIR ROBERT: Was it directly after dinner?

RONNIE: Yes, I think so.

SIR ROBERT: What did you do after leaving the locker room?

RONNIE: I've told you. I went for permission to go to the post office.

SIR ROBERT: What time was that?

RONNIE: About a quarter past two.

SIR ROBERT: Dinner is over at a quarter to two. Which means that you were alone in the locker room for half an hour?

RONNIE: I wasn't there all that time——

SIR ROBERT: How long were you there?

RONNIE: About five minutes.

SIR ROBERT: What were you doing for the other twenty-five?

RONNIE: I don't remember.

SIR ROBERT: It's odd that your memory is so good about some things and so bad about others——

RONNIE: Perhaps I waited outside the C.O.'s office.

SIR ROBERT (*with searing sarcasm*): Perhaps you waited outside the C.O.'s office. And perhaps no one saw you there, either?

RONNIE: No. I don't think they did.

SIR ROBERT: What were you thinking about outside the C.O.'s office for twenty-five minutes?

RONNIE (*wildly*): I don't even know if I was there. I can't remember. Perhaps I wasn't there at all.

SIR ROBERT: No. Perhaps you were still in the locker room rifling Elliot's locker——

ARTHUR (*indignantly*): Sir Robert, I must ask you——

SIR ROBERT: Quiet!

RONNIE: I remember now. I remember. Someone did see me outside the C.O.'s office. A chap called Casey. I remember I spoke to him.

SIR ROBERT: What did you say?

RONNIE: I said: "Come down to the post office with me. I'm going to cash a postal order."

SIR ROBERT (*triumphantly*): *Cash* a postal order.

RONNIE: I mean get.

SIR ROBERT: You said cash. Why did you say cash if you meant get?

RONNIE: I don't know.

SIR ROBERT: I suggest cash was the truth.

RONNIE: No, no. It wasn't. It wasn't really. You're muddling me.

SIR ROBERT: You seem easily muddled. How many other lies have you told?

RONNIE: None. Really I haven't.

SIR ROBERT (*bending forward malevolently*): I suggest your whole testimony is a lie.

RONNIE: No! It's the truth.

SIR ROBERT: I suggest there is barely one single word of truth in anything you have said either to me, or to the Judge Advocate or to the Commander. I suggest that you broke into Elliot's locker, that you stole the postal order for five shillings belonging to Elliot, and you cashed it by means of forging his name.

RONNIE (*wailing*): I didn't. I didn't.

SIR ROBERT: I suggest you did it for a joke, meaning to give Elliot the five shillings back, but that when you met him and he said he had reported the matter that you got frightened and decided to keep quiet.

RONNIE: No, no, no. It isn't true.

SIR ROBERT: I suggest that by continuing to deny your guilt you are causing great hardship to your own family, and considerable annoyance to high and important persons in this country——

CATHERINE (*on her feet*): That's a disgraceful thing to say!

ARTHUR (*rising*): I agree.

SIR ROBERT (*leaning forward and glaring at* RONNIE *with utmost venom*): I suggest that the time has at last come for you to undo some of the misery you have caused by confessing to us all now that you are a forger, a liar and a thief.

(GRACE *rises, crosses swiftly to* RONNIE *and envelops him.*)

RONNIE (*in tears*): I'm not! I'm not! I'm not! I didn't do it.

ARTHUR: This is outrageous, sir.

(DESMOND *crosses above* SIR ROBERT *to the table and collects the documents.* JOHN *enters. He is dressed in evening clothes.*)

JOHN: Kate, dear, I'm late. I'm terribly sorry——

(*He stops short as he takes in the scene.* RONNIE *is sobbing hysterically on his mother's breast.* ARTHUR *and* CATHERINE *are glaring indignantly at* SIR ROBERT, *who is putting his papers together.*)

SIR ROBERT (*to* DESMOND): Can I drop you anywhere? My car is at the door.

DESMOND: Er—no—I thank you.

SIR ROBERT (*carelessly*): Well, send all this stuff round to my chambers to-morrow morning, will you?

DESMOND: But—but will you need it now?

SIR ROBERT: Oh, yes. The boy is plainly innocent. I accept the brief.

(SIR ROBERT *bows to* ARTHUR *and* CATHERINE *and walks languidly to the door past the bewildered* JOHN, *to whom he gives a polite nod as he goes out.* RONNIE *continues to sob hysterically.*)

QUICK CURTAIN

ACT II

SCENE I

The same. Nine months later. An evening in January, about ten-thirty p.m.

ARTHUR *is sitting in his armchair, reading aloud from an evening paper. Listening to him are* RONNIE *and* GRACE, *though neither of them seems to be doing so with much concentration.* RONNIE *is sitting in an armchair, finding it hard to keep his eyes open, and* GRACE, *darning some vests, has evidently other and, to her, more important matters on her mind.*

ARTHUR (*reading*): "——the Admiralty, during the whole of this long-drawn-out dispute have at no time acted hastily or ill-advisedly, and it is a matter of mere histrionic hyperbole for the Right Honourable and learned gentleman opposite to characterize the conduct of my department as that of callousness so inhuman as to amount to deliberate malice towards the boy Winslow. Such unfounded accusations I can well choose to ignore. (An Honourable Member: "You can't.") Honourable Members opposite may interrupt as much as they please, but I repeat—there is nothing whatever that the Admiralty has done, or failed to do, in the case of this cadet for which I, as First Lord, need to apologize. (Further Opposition interruptions.)" (*He stops reading and looks up.*) I must say it looks as if the First Lord's having rather a rough passage——
(ARTHUR *breaks off, noticing* RONNIE'S *head has fallen back on the cushions and he is asleep.*)
(At RONNIE) I trust my reading isn't keeping you awake.
            (*There is no answer.*)
I say I trust my reading isn't keeping you awake !
            (*Again there is no answer.*)
(*helplessly*) Grace !

GRACE: My poor sleepy little lamb! It's long past his bed-time, Arthur.

ARTHUR: Grace, dear—at this very moment your poor sleepy little lamb is the subject of a very violent and heated debate in the House of Commons. I should have thought that, in the circumstances, it might have been possible for him to contrive to stay awake for a few minutes past his bedtime——

GRACE: I expect he's over-excited——

(ARTHUR and GRACE both look at the tranquilly oblivious form.)

ARTHUR: A picture of over-excitement. (Sharply) Ronnie!
(There is no answer.)
Ronnie!

RONNIE (opening his eyes): Yes, Father?

ARTHUR: I am reading the account of the debate. Would you like to listen, or would you rather go to bed?

RONNIE: Oh, I'd like to listen, of course, Father. I was listening, too, only I had my eyes shut——

ARTHUR: Very well. (He reads) "The First Lord continued amid further interruptions: the chief point of criticism against the Admiralty appears to centre in the purely legal question of the Petition of Right brought by Mr. Arthur Winslow and the Admiralty's demurrer thereto. Sir Robert Morton has made great play with his eloquent reference to the liberty of the individual menaced, as he puts it, by the new despotism of bureaucracy— and I was as moved as any Honourable Member opposite by his resonant use of the words: Let Right be done—the time-honoured phrase with which, in his opinion, the Attorney-General should, without question, have en-dorsed Mr. Winslow's Petition of Right. Nevertheless the matter is not nearly as simple as he appears to imagine.

Cadet Ronald Winslow was a servant of the Crown, and has therefore no more right than any other member of His Majesty's forces—to sue the Crown in open court. To allow him to do so—would undoubtedly raise the most dangerous precedents. There is no doubt whatever in my mind that in certain cases private rights may have to be sacrificed for the public good——" (*He looks up.*) And what other excuse, pray, did Charles I make for ship money?

(RONNIE, *after a manful attempt to keep his eyes open by self-pinchings and other devices, has once more succumbed to oblivion.*)

(*Sharply*) Ronnie! Ronnie!

(RONNIE *stirs, turns over, and slides more comfortably into the cushions.*)

Would you believe it!

GRACE: He's dead tired. I'd better take him up to his bed——

ARTHUR: No, if he must sleep, let him sleep there.

GRACE: Oh, but he'd be much more comfy in his little bed——

ARTHUR: I dare say, but the debate continues and until it's ended the cause of it all will certainly not make himself comfy in his little bed.

(VIOLET *comes in.*)

VIOLET (*to* ARTHUR): There are three more reporters in the hall, sir. Want to see you very urgently. Shall I let them in?

ARTHUR: No. Certainly not. I issued a statement yesterday. Until the debate is over I have nothing more to say.

VIOLET: Yes, sir. That's what I told them, but they wouldn't go.

ARTHUR: Well, make them. Use force, if necessary.

VIOLET: Yes, sir. And shall I cut some sandwiches for Miss Catherine, as she missed her dinner?

GRACE: Yes, Violet. Good idea.

VIOLET: Yes, m'm.

(VIOLET *goes out*.)

VIOLET (*as she closes the door; to unseen persons in the hall*): No. No good. No more statements.

ARTHUR: Grace, dear——

GRACE: Yes?

ARTHUR: I fancy this might be a good opportunity of talking to Violet.

GRACE (*quite firmly*): No, dear.

ARTHUR: Meaning that it isn't a good opportunity? Or meaning that you have no intention at all of ever talking to Violet?

GRACE: I'll do it one day, Arthur. To-morrow, perhaps. Not now.

ARTHUR: I believe you'd do better to grasp the nettle. Delay only adds to your worries——

GRACE (*bitterly*): My worries? What do you know about my worries?

ARTHUR: A good deal, Grace. But I feel they would be a lot lessened if you faced the situation squarely.

GRACE: It's easy for you to talk, Arthur. You don't have to do it.

ARTHUR: I will, if you like.

GRACE: No, dear.

ARTHUR: If you explain the dilemma to her carefully—if you even show her the figures I jotted down for you yesterday—I venture to think you won't find her unreasonable.

GRACE: It won't be easy for her to find another place.

ARTHUR: We'll give her an excellent reference.

GRACE: That won't alter the fact that she's never been properly trained as a parlourmaid and—well—you know yourself how we're always having to explain her to people. No, Arthur, I don't mind how many figures she's shown, it's a brutal thing to do.

ARTHUR: Facts are brutal things.

GRACE (*a shade hysterically*): Facts? I don't think I know what facts are any more——

ARTHUR: The facts at this moment are that we have a half of the income we had a year ago, and we're living at nearly the same rate. However you look at it that's bad economics——

GRACE: I'm not talking about economics, Arthur—I'm talking about ordinary, common or garden facts—things we took for granted a year ago and which now don't seem to matter any more.

ARTHUR: Such as?

GRACE (*with rising voice*). Such as a happy home and peace and quiet and an ordinary respectable life, and some sort of future for us and our children. In the last year you've thrown all that overboard, Arthur. There's your return for it, I suppose—(*she indicates the headline in the paper*) —and it's all very exciting and important, I'm sure, but it doesn't bring back any of the things that we've lost——
              (RONNIE *stirs in his sleep.*)
(*She lowers her voice*) I can only pray to God that you know what you're doing.

ARTHUR (*after a pause; rising with difficulty*): I know exactly what I'm doing, Grace. I'm going to publish my son's innocence before the world, and for that end I am not prepared to weigh the cost.

GRACE: But the cost may be out of all proportion——

ARTHUR: It may be. That doesn't concern me. I hate heroics, Grace, but you force me to say this. An injustice has been done. I am going to set it right, and there is no sacrifice in the world I am not prepared to make in order to do so.

GRACE (*with sudden violence*): Oh, I wish I could see the sense of it all! (*She points to* RONNIE) He's perfectly happy, at a good school, doing very well. No one need ever have known about Osborne, if you hadn't gone and shouted it out to the whole world. As it is, whatever happens now, he'll go through the rest of his life as the boy in that Winslow case—the boy who stole that postal order——

ARTHUR (*grimly*): The boy who didn't steal that postal order.

GRACE (*wearily*): What's the difference? When millions are talking and gossiping about him a " did " or a " didn't " hardly matters. The Winslow boy is bad enough. You talk about sacrificing everything for him; but when he's grown up he won't thank you for it, Arthur—even though you've given your life to—publish his innocence as you call it.
     (ARTHUR *makes an impatient gesture.*)
Yes, Arthur—your life. You talk gaily about arthritis and a touch of gout and old age and the rest of it, but you know as well as any of the doctors what really is the matter with you. (*Nearly in tears*) You're destroying yourself, Arthur, and me and your family besides—and for what I'd like to know? I've asked you and Kate to tell me a hundred times—but you never can. For what, Arthur?

ARTHUR (*quietly*): For Justice, Grace.

GRACE : That sounds very noble. Are you sure it's true? Are you sure it isn't just plain pride and self-importance and sheer brute stubbornness?

ARTHUR (*putting a hand out to her*): No, Grace. I don't think it is. I really don't think it is——

GRACE : No. This time I'm not going to cry and say I'm sorry, and make it all up again. I can stand anything if there is a reason for it. But for no reason at all, it's unfair to ask so much of me. It's unfair . . .

(GRACE *breaks down, moves swiftly to the door and goes out.* RONNIE *opens his eyes.* ARTHUR *makes a move as though he is about to follow* GRACE.)

RONNIE : What's the matter, Father?

ARTHUR : Your mother is a little upset.

RONNIE (*drowsily*): Why? Aren't things going well?

ARTHUR : Oh yes. (*Murmuring*) Very well. Very well, indeed.
(RONNIE *contentedly closes his eyes again.* ARTHUR *sits down painfully.*)
(*Gently*) You'd better go to bed now, Ronnie. You'll be more comfortable.
(*He sees* RONNIE *is asleep again. He makes as if to wake him, but then shrugs his shoulders.* VIOLET *comes in with a plate of sandwiches, which she puts on the table, and a letter on a salver which she hands to* ARTHUR. *He puts it down without opening it.*)
Thank you, Violet. Oh, Violet——

VIOLET (*placidly*): Yes, sir?

ARTHUR : How long have you been with us?

VIOLET : Twenty-four years come April, sir.

ARTHUR : As long as that?

VIOLET: Yes, sir. Miss Kate was that high when I first came (*she indicates a small child*) and Mr. Dickie hadn't even been thought of——

ARTHUR: I remember your coming to us, now. I remember it well. What do you think of this case, Violet?

VIOLET: A fine old rumpus that is, and no mistake.

ARTHUR: It is, isn't it? A fine old rumpus.

VIOLET: There was a bit in the *Evening News*. Did you read it, sir?

ARTHUR: No. What did it say?

VIOLET: Oh, about how it was a fuss about nothing and a shocking waste of the Government's time, but how it was a good thing all the same because it could only happen in England——

ARTHUR: There seems to be a certain lack of logic in that argument——

VIOLET: Well, perhaps they put it a bit different, sir. Still, that's what it said all right. And when you think it's all because of our Master Ronnie I have to laugh about it sometimes, I really do. Wasting the Government's time at his age! I never did. Well, wonders will never cease.

ARTHUR: I know. Wonders will never cease.

VIOLET: Well—would that be all, sir?

ARTHUR (*after a slight pause*): Yes, Violet. That'll be all.

(CATHERINE *comes in.*)

CATHERINE: Good evening, Violet.

VIOLET: Good evening, Miss.

(*She goes out.*)

80

CATHERINE: Hello, Father. (*She kisses him. She indicates* RONNIE) An Honourable Member described *that* this evening as a piteous little figure, crying aloud to humanity for justice and redress. I wish he could see him now.

ARTHUR (*testily*): It's long past his bed-time. What's happened? Is the debate over?

CATHERINE: As good as. The First Lord gave an assurance that in future there would be no enquiry at Osborne or Dartmouth without informing the parents first. That seemed to satisfy most Members——

ARTHUR: But what about our case? Is he going to allow us a fair trial?

CATHERINE: Apparently not.

ARTHUR: But that's iniquitous. I thought he would be forced to——

CATHERINE: I thought so, too. The House evidently thought otherwise.

ARTHUR: Will there be a division?

CATHERINE: There may be. If there is the Government will win.

ARTHUR: What is the motion?

CATHERINE: To reduce the First Lord's salary by a hundred pounds. (*With a faint smile*) Naturally no one really wants to do that. (*She sees the sandwiches*) Are those for me?

ARTHUR: Yes.
    (CATHERINE *starts to eat the sandwiches.*)
So we're back where we started, then?

CATHERINE: It looks like it.

ARTHUR: The debate has done us no good at all?

CATHERINE: It's aired the case a little, perhaps. A few more thousand people will say to each other at breakfast to-morrow: " That boy ought to be allowed a fair trial."

ARTHUR: What's the good of that, if they can't make themselves heard?

CATHERINE: I think they can—given time.

ARTHUR: Given time? (*He pauses.*) But didn't Sir Robert make any protest when the First Lord refused a trial?

CATHERINE: Not a verbal protest. Something far more spectacular and dramatic. He'd had his feet on the Treasury table and his hat over his eyes, during most of the First Lord's speech—and suddenly got up very deliberately, glared at the First Lord, threw a whole bundle of notes on the floor, and stalked out of the House. It made a magnificent effect. If I hadn't known I could have sworn he was genuinely indignant——

ARTHUR: Of course he was genuinely indignant. So would any man of feeling be.

CATHERINE: Sir Robert, Father dear, is not a man of feeling. I don't think any emotion at all can stir that fishy heart——

ARTHUR: Except, perhaps, a single-minded love of justice.

CATHERINE: Nonsense. A single-minded love of Sir Robert Morton.

ARTHUR: You're very ungrateful to him, considering all he's done for us these last months——

CATHERINE: I'm not ungrateful, Father. He's been wonderful—I admit it freely. No one could have fought a harder fight.

ARTHUR: Well, then——

CATHERINE: It's only his motives I question. At least I don't question them at all. I know them.

ARTHUR: What are they?

CATHERINE: First—publicity—you know—"Look at me, the staunch defender of the little man"—and then second—a nice popular stick to beat the Government with. Both very useful to an ambitious man. Luckily for him we've provided them.

ARTHUR: Luckily for us too, Kate.

CATHERINE: Oh, I agree. But don't fool yourself about him, Father, for all that. The man is a fish, a hard, cold-blooded, supercilious, sneering fish.

(VIOLET *enters.*)

VIOLET (*announcing*): Sir Robert Morton.

(CATHERINE *chokes over her sandwich.* SIR ROBERT *comes in.*)

SIR ROBERT: Good evening.

CATHERINE (*still choking*): Good evening.

SIR ROBERT: Something gone down the wrong way?

CATHERINE: Yes.

SIR ROBERT: May I assist. (*He pats her on the back.*)

CATHERINE: Thank you.

SIR ROBERT (*to* ARTHUR): Good evening, sir. I thought I would call, and give you an account of the day's proceedings, but I see your daughter has forestalled me.

CATHERINE: Did you know I was in the gallery?

SIR ROBERT (*gallantly*): In such a charming hat, how could I have missed you?

83

ARTHUR: It was very good of you to call, sir, nevertheless.

SIR ROBERT (*seeing* RONNIE): Ah. The *casus belli*—dormant——

(ARTHUR *rises and stretches across to wake* RONNIE.)

No, no, I beg of you. Please do not disturb his innocent slumbers.

CATHERINE: *Innocent* slumbers?

SIR ROBERT: Exactly. Besides, I fear since our first encounter he is, rather pardonably, a trifle nervous of me.

CATHERINE: Will you betray a technical secret, Sir Robert? What happened in that first examination to make you so sure of his innocence?

SIR ROBERT: Three things. First of all, he made far too many damaging admissions. A guilty person would have been much more careful—much more on his guard. Secondly, I laid him a trap; and thirdly left him a loophole. Anyone who was guilty would have fallen into the one and darted through the other. He did neither.

CATHERINE: The trap was to ask him suddenly what time Elliot put the postal order in his locker. Wasn't it?

SIR ROBERT: Yes.

ARTHUR: And the loophole?

SIR ROBERT: I then suggested to him that he had stolen the postal order for a joke—which, had he been guilty, he would surely have admitted to as being the lesser of two evils.

CATHERINE: I see. It was very cleverly thought out.

SIR ROBERT (*with a little bow*): Thank you.

ARTHUR: May we offer you some refreshment, Sir Robert? A whisky and soda?

SIR ROBERT: No, thank you. Nothing at all.

ARTHUR: My daughter has told me of your demonstration during the First Lord's speech. She described it as— magnificent.

SIR ROBERT (*with a glance at* CATHERINE): Did she? That was good of her. It's a very old trick, you know. I've done it many times in the Courts. It's nearly always surprisingly effective——
(CATHERINE *catches her father's eye and nods triumphantly.*)
(*To* CATHERINE) Was the First Lord at all put out by it— did you notice?

CATHERINE: How could he have failed to be? (*She rises and crosses to* ARTHUR) I wish you could have seen it, Father —it was—— (*She notices the letter on the table beside* ARTHUR *and snatches it up with a sudden gesture. She examines the envelope.*) When did this come?

ARTHUR: A few minutes ago. Do you know the writing?

CATHERINE: Yes. (*She puts the letter back on the table.*)

ARTHUR: Whose is it?

CATHERINE: I shouldn't bother to read it, if I were you.

(ARTHUR *looks at her, puzzled, then takes up the letter.*)

ARTHUR (*to* SIR ROBERT): Will you forgive me?

SIR ROBERT: Of course.

(ARTHUR *opens the letter and begins to read.* CATHERINE *watches him for a moment; then she turns with a certain forced liveliness to* SIR ROBERT.)

CATHERINE: Well, what do you think the next step should be?

SIR ROBERT: I have already been considering that, Miss Winslow—I believe that perhaps the best plan would be to renew our efforts to get the Director of Public Prosecutions to act.

CATHERINE (*with one eye on her father*): But do you think there's any chance of that?

SIR ROBERT: Oh, yes. In the main it will chiefly be a question of making ourselves a confounded nuisance——

CATHERINE: We've certainly done that quite successfully so far, thanks to you——

SIR ROBERT (*suavely*): Ah. That is perhaps the only quality I was born with—the ability to make myself a confounded nuisance. (*He, too, has his eyes on* ARTHUR, *sensing something amiss.*)

(ARTHUR *finishes reading the letter.*)

CATHERINE (*with false vivacity*): Father—Sir Robert thinks we might get the Director of Public Prosecutions to act.

ARTHUR: What?

SIR ROBERT: We were discussing how to proceed with the case——

ARTHUR: The case? (*He stares a little blankly, from the one to the other*) Yes. We must think of that, mustn't we? (*He pauses*) How to proceed with the case? (*To* SIR ROBERT, *abruptly*) I'm afraid I don't think, all things considered, that much purpose would be served by going on—— (*He hands the letter to* CATHERINE.)

(SIR ROBERT *stares blankly at* ARTHUR. CATHERINE *reads the letter.*)

SIR ROBERT (*with a sudden change of tone*): Of course we must go on.

ARTHUR (*in a low voice*): It is not for you to choose, sir. The choice is mine.

SIR ROBERT (*harshly*): Then you must reconsider it. To give up now would be insane.

ARTHUR: Insane? My sanity has already been called in question to-night—for carrying the case as far as I have.

SIR ROBERT: Whatever the contents of that letter, or whatever has happened to make you lose heart, I insist that we continue the fight——

ARTHUR: Insist? We? It is my fight—my fight alone—and it is for me alone to judge when the time has come to give up.

SIR ROBERT (*violently*): Give up? But why give up? In Heaven's name, man, why?

ARTHUR (*slowly*): I have made many sacrifices for this case. Some of them I had no right to make, but I made them none the less. But there is a limit, and I have reached it. I am sorry, Sir Robert. More sorry, perhaps, than you are, but the Winslow case is now closed.

SIR ROBERT: Balderdash!

(ARTHUR *looks surprised at this unparliamentary expression.* CATHERINE *has read, and re-read the letter, and now breaks the silence in a calm, methodical voice.*)

CATHERINE: My father doesn't mean what he says, Sir Robert.

SIR ROBERT: I'm glad to hear it.

CATHERINE: Perhaps I should explain that this letter——

ARTHUR: No, Kate.

CATHERINE: Sir Robert knows so much about our family affairs, Father, I don't see it will matter much if he learns a little more. (To SIR ROBERT) This letter is from a certain Colonel Watherstone who is the father of the man I'm engaged to. We've always known he was opposed to the case, so it really comes as no surprise. In it he says that our efforts to discredit the Admiralty in the House of Commons to-day have resulted merely in making the name of Winslow a nation-wide laughing-stock. I think that's his phrase. (*She consults the letter*) Yes. That's right. " A nation-wide laughing-stock."

SIR ROBERT: I don't care for his English——

CATHERINE: It's not very good, is it? He goes on to say that unless my father will give him a firm undertaking to drop this "whining and reckless agitation"—I suppose he means the case—he will exert every bit of influence he has over his son to prevent his marrying me.

SIR ROBERT: I see. An ultimatum.

CATHERINE: Yes—but a pointless one.

SIR ROBERT: He has no influence over his son?

CATHERINE: Oh, yes. A little, naturally. But his son is of age, and his own master——

SIR ROBERT: Is he dependent on his father for money?

CATHERINE: He gets an allowance. But he can live perfectly well—we can both live perfectly well, without it.

(SIR ROBERT *stares hard at* CATHERINE, *then turns abruptly and crosses to* ARTHUR.)

SIR ROBERT: Well, sir?

ARTHUR: I'm afraid I can't go back on what I have already said. I will give you a decision in a few days——

SIR ROBERT: Your daughter seems prepared to take the risk——

ARTHUR: I am not. Not, at least, until I know how great a risk it is——

SIR ROBERT (*turning to* CATHERINE): How do you estimate the risk, Miss Winslow?

(CATHERINE, *for all her bravado, is plainly scared. She is engaged in lighting a cigarette as* SIR ROBERT *asks his question.*)

CATHERINE (*after a pause*): Negligible.

(SIR ROBERT *stares at her again. Feeling his eyes on her,*
CATHERINE *returns his glance defiantly. There is a pause.*)

SIR ROBERT (*returning abruptly to his languid manner*): I
see. May I take a cigarette too?

CATHERINE: Yes, of course. I thought you didn't smoke.

SIR ROBERT: Only occasionally. (*He takes a cigarette. To*
ARTHUR) I really must apologize to you, sir, for speaking
to you as I did just now. It was unforgivable.

ARTHUR: Not at all. You were upset at giving up the case
—and, to be frank, I liked you for it——

SIR ROBERT (*with a deprecating gesture*): It has been rather
a tiring day. The House of Commons is a peculiarly
exhausting place, you know. Too little ventilation and
far too much hot air—I really am most truly sorry.

ARTHUR (*dismissing the matter*): Please. (*He sits in his*
chair.)

SIR ROBERT (*carelessly*): Of course, you must decide about
the case as you wish. (*To* CATHERINE) That really is a
most charming hat, Miss Winslow——

CATHERINE: I'm glad you like it.

SIR ROBERT: It seems decidedly wrong to me that a lady
of your political persuasion should be allowed to adorn
herself with such a very feminine allurement. It really
looks so awfully like trying to have the best of both
worlds——

CATHERINE: I'm not a militant, you know, Sir Robert. I
don't go about breaking shop windows with a hammer or
pouring acid down pillar boxes.

SIR ROBERT (*languidly*): I am truly glad to hear it. Both
those activities would be highly unsuitable in that
hat——

89

(CATHERINE *glares at him, but suppresses an angry retort.*) I have never yet fully grasped what active steps you do take to propagate your cause, Miss Winslow?

CATHERINE (*shortly*): I'm an organizing secretary at the West London Branch of the Women's Suffrage Association.

SIR ROBERT: Indeed? Is the work hard?

CATHERINE: Very.

SIR ROBERT: But not, I should imagine, particularly lucrative.

CATHERINE: The work is voluntary and unpaid.

SIR ROBERT (*murmuring*): Dear me! What sacrifice you young ladies seem prepared to make for your convictions——

(VIOLET *enters.*)

VIOLET (*to* CATHERINE): Mr. Watherstone is in the hall, Miss. Says he would like to have a word with you in private—most particular——

(*There is a pause.*)

CATHERINE: Oh. I'll come out to him——

ARTHUR: No. See him in here. (*He begins to struggle out of his chair*) You wouldn't mind coming to the dining-room, would you, Sir Robert, for a moment?

SIR ROBERT: Not in the least.

CATHERINE: All right, Violet.

VIOLET (*speaking into the hall*): Will you come in, sir?

(JOHN *comes in. He is looking depressed and anxious.* CATHERINE *greets him with a smile, which he returns only half-heartedly. This exchange is lost on* ARTHUR,

who has his back to them, but not on SIR ROBERT.
VIOLET *goes out.*)

CATHERINE: Hello, John.

JOHN: Hullo. (*To* ARTHUR) Good evening, sir.

ARTHUR: Good evening. (*He continues towards the dining-
room door.*)

CATHERINE: I don't think you've met Sir Robert Morton.

JOHN: No, I haven't. How do you do, sir?

SIR ROBERT: How do you do? (*He sizes him up quickly.
To* ARTHUR) I think you promised me a whisky and soda.
(*He turns to* JOHN) May I offer my very belated
congratulations?

JOHN: Congratulations? Oh, yes. Thank you.
(ARTHUR *and* SIR ROBERT *go into the dining-room. There
is a pause.* CATHERINE *is watching* JOHN *with an
anxious expression.* JOHN *moves down to* RONNIE.)
Is he asleep?

CATHERINE: Yes.

JOHN (*still looking at* RONNIE): Sure he's not shamming?

CATHERINE: Yes.

JOHN (*after a pause*): My father's written your father a
letter.

CATHERINE: I know. I've read it.

JOHN: Oh!

CATHERINE: Did you?

JOHN: Yes. He showed it to me.
(*There is a pause.* JOHN *is carefully not looking at*
CATHERINE.)
Well, what's his answer?

CATHERINE: My father? I don't suppose he'll send one.

JOHN: You think he'll ignore it?

CATHERINE: Isn't that the best answer to blackmail?

JOHN (*muttering*): It was damned high-handed of the old man, I admit.

CATHERINE: High-handed?

JOHN: I tried to get him not to send it.

CATHERINE: I'm glad.

JOHN: The trouble is—he's perfectly serious.

CATHERINE: I never thought he wasn't.

JOHN: If your father does decide to go on with the case, I'm very much afraid he'll do everything he threatens.

CATHERINE: Forbid the match?

JOHN: Yes.

CATHERINE (*almost pleadingly*): Isn't that rather an empty threat, John?

JOHN (*slowly*): Well, there's always the allowance.

CATHERINE (*dully*): Yes, I see. There's always the allowance——

JOHN: I tell you, Kate darling, this is going to need damned careful handling; otherwise we'll find ourselves in the soup.

CATHERINE: Without your allowance would we be in the soup?

JOHN: And without your settlement? My dear old girl, of course we would. Dash it all, I can't even live on my pay as it is, but with two of us——

CATHERINE: I've heard it said that two can live as cheaply as one.

JOHN: Don't you believe it. Two can live as cheaply as two, and that's all there is to it.

CATHERINE: Yes, I see. I didn't know.

JOHN: Unlike you, I have a practical mind, Kate. I'm sorry, but it's no use dashing blindly ahead without thinking of these things first. The problem has got to be faced.

CATHERINE: I'm ready to face it, John. What do you suggest?

JOHN (*cautiously*): Well—I think you should consider very carefully before you take the next step.

CATHERINE: I can assure you we will, John. The question is—what is the next step——

JOHN: Well—this is the way I see it. I'm going to be honest now. I hope you don't mind——

CATHERINE: No. I should welcome it.

JOHN: Your young brother over there pinches or doesn't pinch a five bob postal order. For over a year you and your father fight a magnificent fight on his behalf, and I'm sure everyone admires you for it.

CATHERINE: Your father hardly seems to.

JOHN: Well, he's a diehard, like these old admirals you've been up against. I meant ordinary reasonable people like myself. But now look—you've had two enquiries, the Petition of Right case which the Admiralty had thrown out of court, and the Appeal. And now, good heavens, you've had the whole damned House of Commons getting themselves worked up into a frenzy about it. Surely, darling, that's enough for you? My God! Surely the case can end there?

CATHERINE (*slowly*): Yes. I suppose the case can end there.

JOHN (*pointing to* RONNIE): *He* won't mind.

CATHERINE: No. I know he won't.

JOHN: Look at him! (*He gazes down at* RONNIE) Perfectly happy and content. Not a care in the world. How do you know what's going on in his mind? How can you be so sure he didn't do it?

CATHERINE (*also gazing down at* RONNIE): I'm not so sure he didn't do it.

JOHN (*appalled*): Good Lord! Then why in Heaven's name have you and your father spent all this time and money trying to prove his innocence?

CATHERINE (*quietly*): His innocence or guilt aren't important to me. They are to my father. Not to me. I believe he didn't do it, but I may be wrong. To prove that he didn't do it is of hardly more interest to me than the identity of the college servant, or whoever it was who did it. All that I care about is that people should know that a Government department has ignored a fundamental human right and that it should be forced to acknowledge it. That's all that's important to me, John, but it is terribly important.

JOHN: But, darling, after all those long noble words, it does really resolve itself to a question of a fourteen-year-old boy and a five bob postal order, doesn't it?

CATHERINE: Yes, it does. (*She continues to gaze down at* RONNIE.)

JOHN (*reasonably*): Well now, look. There's a European war blowing up, there's a coal strike on, there's a fair chance of civil war in Ireland, and there's a hundred and one other things on the horizon at the moment that I think you genuinely could call important. And yet, with all that on its mind, the House of Commons takes a whole day to discuss him—(*pointing to* RONNIE) and his bally postal order. Surely you must see that's a little out of proportion——(*He pauses.*)

CATHERINE (*with some spirit*): All I know is, John, that if ever the time comes when the House of Commons has so much on its mind that it can't find time to discuss a Ronnie Winslow and his bally postal order, this country will be a far poorer place than it is now. (*Wearily*) But you needn't go on, John, dear. You've said quite enough. I entirely see your point of view.

JOHN: I don't know whether you realize that all this publicity you're getting is making the name of Winslow a bit of a—well——

CATHERINE (*steadily*): A nation-wide laughing-stock, your father said.

JOHN: Well, that's putting it a bit steep. But people do find the case a bit ridiculous, you know. I mean, I get chaps coming up to me in the mess all the time and saying: "Is it true you're going to marry the Winslow girl? You'd better be careful. You'll find yourself up in front of the House of Lords for pinching the Adjutant's bath." Things like that. They're not awfully funny——

CATHERINE: That's nothing. They're singing a verse about us at the Alhambra—

> "Winslow one day went to Heaven
> And found a poor fellow in quod.
> The fellow said 'I didn't do it',
> So naturally Winslow sued God."

JOHN: Well, darling—you see——

CATHERINE: Yes, I see. (*Quietly*) Do you want to marry me, John?

JOHN: What?

CATHERINE: I said: do you want to marry me?

JOHN: Well, of course I do. You know I do. We've been engaged for over a year now. Have I ever wavered before?

CATHERINE: No, never before.

JOHN (*correcting himself*): I'm not wavering now. Nót a bit—I'm only telling you what I think is the best course for us to take.

CATHERINE: But isn't it already too late? Even if we gave up the case, would you still want to marry—the Winslow girl?

JOHN: All that would blow over in no time.

CATHERINE (*slowly*): And we'd have the allowance——

JOHN: Yes. We would.

CATHERINE: And that's so important——

JOHN (*quietly*): It is, darling. I'm sorry, but you can't shame me into saying it isn't.

CATHERINE: I didn't mean to shame you——

JOHN: Oh yes, you did. I know that tone of voice.

CATHERINE (*humbly*): I'm sorry.

JOHN (*confidently*): Well, now—what's the answer?

CATHERINE (*slowly*): I love you, John, and want to be your wife.

JOHN: Well, then, that's all I want to know. Darling! I was sure nothing so stupid and trivial could possibly come between us.

(*He kisses her. She responds wearily. The telephone rings. After a pause,* CATHERINE *releases herself and lifts the receiver.*)

CATHERINE: Hullo . . . Yes . . . Will you wait a minute? (*She crosses to the dining-room door and calls*): Sir Robert! Someone wants you on the telephone.

(SIR ROBERT *enters from the dining-room.*)

SIR ROBERT: Thank you. I'm sorry to interrupt.

CATHERINE: You didn't. We'd finished our talk.

(SIR ROBERT *looks at her enquiringly. She gives him no sign. He crosses to the telephone.*)

SIR ROBERT (*noticing the sandwiches*): How delicious. May I help myself? (*He takes one and continues to the desk.*)

CATHERINE: Do.

SIR ROBERT (*into the telephone*): Hullo . . . Yes, Michael . . . F. E.? I didn't know he was going to speak . . . I see . . . Go on.

(*The man at the other end of the line speaks for some time.* SIR ROBERT *listens with closed eyelids, munching a sandwich.* ARTHUR *appears in the dining-room doorway.*)

(*At length.*) Thank you, Michael. (*He hangs up the receiver. To* ARTHUR) There has been a most interesting development in the House.

ARTHUR: What?

SIR ROBERT: My secretary tells me that a barrister friend of mine who, quite unknown to me, was interested in the case, got on his feet shortly after nine-thirty and delivered one of the most scathing denunciations of a Government department ever heard in the House. (*To* CATHERINE) What a shame we missed it—his style is quite superb——

ARTHUR: What happened?

SIR ROBERT: The debate revived, of course, and the First Lord, who must have felt himself fairly safe, suddenly found himself under attack from all parts of the House. It appears that rather than risk a division he has this moment given an undertaking that he will instruct the Attorney-General to endorse our Petition of Right. The case of Winslow versus Rex can now therefore come to court.

(*There is a pause.* ARTHUR *and* CATHERINE *stare at him unbelievingly.*)
Well, sir. What are my instructions?

ARTHUR (*slowly*): The decision is no longer mine. You must ask my daughter.

SIR ROBERT (*to* CATHERINE): What are my instructions, Miss Winslow? (*He takes another sandwich.*)

(CATHERINE *looks down at the sleeping* RONNIE. ARTHUR *watches her intently.* SIR ROBERT, *munching sandwich, also looks at her.*)

CATHERINE (*in a flat voice*): Do you need my instructions, Sir Robert? Aren't they already on the Petition? Doesn't it say, "Let Right be Done"?

(JOHN *makes a move of protest towards her. She does not look at him. He turns abruptly to the door.*)

JOHN (*furiously*): Kate!
                              (*There is no answer.*)
Good night.

(JOHN *goes out.* SIR ROBERT, *with languid speculation, watches him go.*)

SIR ROBERT (*his mouth full*): Well then—we must endeavour to see that it is.

(*The front door is heard to slam.*)

QUICK CURTAIN

SCENE II

The same, five months later.

It is a stiflingly hot afternoon in June—*nearly two years less one month since* RONNIE'S *dismissal from Osborne. The french window stands open, and a wheel-chair has been placed just inside. When the* CURTAIN *rises, the stage is empty and the telephone is ringing insistently.*

After a few seconds, DICKIE'S *voice can be heard, calling from the direction of the hall—"* MOTHER *"—"* VIOLET," *to which he gets no reply. He enters. He is carrying a suit-case, and is evidently very hot; his straw hat is pushed on to the back of his head, and he is panting from his exertions. He is wearing a neat, dark blue suit, a sober tie and a stiff collar.*

DICKIE (*in the doorway*): Anybody about? (*He puts down his suitcase by the door and crosses to the desk. Into the telephone*) Hullo . . . No, not senior—junior . . . I don't know where he is . . . *Daily Mail?* . . . No, I'm the brother . . . elder brother—that's right . . . Well, I'm in the banking business . . . That's right. following in Father's footsteps . . . My views on the case? Well, I—I—er—I don't know that I have any, except, I mean, I hope we win and all that . . . No, I haven't been in court. I've only just arrived from Reading . . . Reading . . . Yes. That's where I work . . . Yes, I've come up for the last two days of the trial. Verdict's expected to-morrow, isn't it? . . . Twenty-two, last March . . . Seven years older . . . No. He was thirteen when it happened, but now he's fifteen . . . Well, I suppose if I'm anything I'm a sort of Liberal-Conservative . . . Single . . . No. No immediate prospects. I say, is this at all interesting to you? . . . Well, a perfectly ordinary kid, just like any other—makes a noise, does fretwork, doesn't wash and all that . . . Doesn't wash . . . (*Alarmed*) I say, don't take that too literally. I mean he does, sometimes . . . Yes, all right. Good-bye . . . (*He hangs up the receiver, picks up his suitcase and goes out leaving the door wide open. The telephone rings again. He drops his suitcase in the hall and comes into the room again as* GRACE *enters from the dining-room.*)

GRACE: Oh, hullo, darling. When did you get here? (*She picks up the receiver. Into the telephone*) Everyone out. (*She hangs up the receiver, crosses to* DICKIE *and embraces him.*) You're thinner. I like your new suit.

DICKIE: Straight from Reading's Savile Row. Off the peg at thirty-seven and six. (*He points to the telephone*) I say—does that go on all the time?

GRACE: All blessed day. The last four days it simply hasn't stopped.

DICKIE: I had to fight my way in through an army of reporters and people—— (*He takes his hat off and drops it on a chair.*)

GRACE: Yes, I know. You didn't say anything, I hope, Dickie dear. It's better not to say a word——

DICKIE: I don't think I said anything much . . . (*Carelessly*) Oh, yes. I did say that I personally thought he did it.

GRACE (*horrified*): Dickie! You didn't!
(DICKIE *smiles at her.*)
Oh, I see. It's a joke. You mustn't say things like that, even in fun, Dickie dear—— (*She goes to the door and closes it.*)

DICKIE: How's it all going?

GRACE: I don't know. I've been there all four days now and I've hardly understood a word that's going on. Kate says the judge is against us, but he seems a charming old gentleman to me. (*Faintly shocked*) Sir Robert's so rude to him——
(*The telephone rings.* GRACE *answers it automatically.*)
Nobody in. (*And hangs up. She goes to the french window and calls*): Arthur! Lunch! I'll come straight down. Dickie's here. (*To Dickie*) Kate takes the morning session, then she comes home and relieves me with

Father, and I go to the court in the afternoons, so you can come with me as soon as she's in.

DICKIE: Will there be room for me?

GRACE: Oh yes. They reserve places for the family. You never saw such crowds in all your life. And such excitement! Cheers and applause and people being turned out. It's thrilling—you'll love it, Dickie.

DICKIE: Well—if I don't understand a word——

GRACE: Oh, that doesn't matter. They all get so terribly worked up—you find yourself getting worked up, too. Sir Robert and the Attorney-General go at each other hammer and tongs—you wait and hear them—all about Petitions and demurrers and prerogatives and things. Nothing to do with Ronnie at all—seems to me——

DICKIE: How did Ronnie get on in the witness box?

GRACE: Two days he was cross-examined. Two whole days, Imagine it, the poor little pet. I must say he didn't seem to mind much. He said two days with the Attorney-General wasn't nearly as bad as two minutes with Sir Robert. Kate says he made a very good impression with the jury——

DICKIE: How is Kate, Mother?

GRACE: Oh, all right. You heard about John, I suppose——

DICKIE: Yes. That's what I meant. How has she taken it?

GRACE: You never can tell with Kate. She never lets you know what she's feeling. We all think he's behaved very badly——

(ARTHUR *appears at the french window. He is walking very groggily, with the aid of a stick.*)

Arthur! You shouldn't have come up those steps by yourself.

ARTHUR: I had little alternative.

GRACE: I'm sorry, dear. I was talking to Dickie. (*She helps* ARTHUR *into the wheelchair.*)

ARTHUR: Oh, hullo, Dickie. How are you? (*He works the chair to the corner of the desk.*)

(GRACE *puts* ARTHUR'S *stick by the side of the piano.*)

DICKIE (*shaking hands*): Very well, thank you, Father.

ARTHUR: I've been forced to adopt this ludicrous form of propulsion. I apologize. You look very well. A trifle thinner, perhaps——

DICKIE: Hard work, Father.

ARTHUR: Or late hours.

DICKIE: You can't keep late hours in Reading.

ARTHUR: You could keep late hours anywhere. I've had quite a good report about you from Mr. Lamb.

DICKIE: Good egg! He's a decent old stick, the old baalamb. I took him racing last Saturday. Had the time of his life and lost his shirt.

ARTHUR: Did he? I have no doubt that, given the chance, you'll succeed in converting the entire Reading branch of the Westminster Bank into a bookmaking establishment. Mr. Lamb says you've joined the territorials.

DICKIE: Yes, Father.

ARTHUR: Why have you done that?

DICKIE: Well, from all accounts there is a fair chance of a bit of a scrap quite soon. If there is I don't want it to be all over before I can get in on it——

ARTHUR: If there is what you call a scrap you'll do far better to stay in the bank——

DICKIE: Oh no, Father. I mean, the bank's all right—but still—a chap can't help looking forward to a bit of a change—I can always go back to the bank afterwards——

(*The telephone rings.* ARTHUR *takes the receiver off and puts it down on the desk.*)

GRACE: Oh no, dear, you can't do that.

ARTHUR: Why not?

GRACE: It annoys the exchange.

ARTHUR: I prefer to annoy the exchange than have the exchange annoy me. Catherine's late. She was in at half-past one yesterday.

GRACE: Perhaps they're taking the lunch interval later to-day.

ARTHUR: Lunch interval? This isn't a cricket match. (*He looks at her*) Nor, may I say, is it a matinee at the Gaiety. Why are you wearing that highly unsuitable get-up?

GRACE: Don't you like it, dear? I think it is Mme. Dupont's best.

ARTHUR: Grace—your son is facing a charge of theft and forgery——

GRACE: Oh dear! It's so difficult! I simply can't be seen in the same old dress, day after day! (*A thought strikes her*) I tell you what, Arthur. I'll wear my black coat and skirt to-morrow—for the verdict.

ARTHUR (*glares at her, helplessly, then turns his chair towards the dining-room*): Did you say my lunch was ready?

GRACE: Yes, dear. It's only cold. I did the salad myself. Violet and cook are at the trial.

DICKIE: Is Violet still with you? She was under sentence last time I saw you——

GRACE: She's been under sentence for the last six months,

poor thing—only she doesn't know it. Neither your father nor I have the courage to tell her——

ARTHUR (*stopping at the door*): I have the courage to tell her.

GRACE: It's funny that you don't then, dear.

ARTHUR: I will.

GRACE (*hastily*): No, no, you mustn't. When it's to be done, I'll do it.

ARTHUR: You see, Dickie? These taunts of cowardice are daily flung at my head; but should I take them up I'm forbidden to move in the matter. Such is the logic of women.

(ARTHUR *wheels himself into the dining-room.* DICKIE, *who has been holding the door open, closes it after him.*)

DICKIE: How is he?
        (GRACE *shakes her head quietly.*)
Will you take him away after the trial?

GRACE: He's promised to go into a nursing home.

DICKIE: Do you think he will?

GRACE: How do I know? He'll probably find some new excuse.

DICKIE: But surely, if he loses this time, he's lost for good, hasn't he?

GRACE (*slowly*): So they say, Dickie dear—I can only hope it's true.

DICKIE: How did you keep him away from the trial?

GRACE: Kate and Sir Robert together. He wouldn't listen to me or the doctor.

DICKIE: Poor old Mother! You must have been having a pretty rotten time of it, one way and another——

GRACE: I've said my say, Dickie. He knows what I think.

Not that he cares. He never has—all his life. Anyway,
I've given up worrying. He's always said he knew what
he was doing. It's my job to try and pick up the pieces,
I suppose.

(CATHERINE *enters.*)

CATHERINE: Lord! The heat! Mother, can't you get rid of
those reporters—Hullo, Dickie.

DICKIE: Hullo, Kate. (*He embraces her.*)

CATHERINE: Come to be in at the death?

DICKIE: Is that what it's going to be?

CATHERINE: Looks like it. I could cheerfully strangle that
old brute of a judge, Mother. He's dead against us.

GRACE: Oh, dear!

CATHERINE: Sir Robert's very worried. He said the
Attorney-General's speech made a great impression on
the jury. I must say it was very clever. To listen to him
yesterday you would have thought that a verdict for
Ronnie would simultaneously cause a mutiny in the
Royal Navy and triumphant jubilation in Berlin.

(*The dining-room door opens and* ARTHUR *appears in
the opening in his chair.*)

ARTHUR: You're late, Catherine.

CATHERINE: I know, Father, I'm sorry. There was such a
huge crowd outside as well as inside the court that I
couldn't get a cab. And I stayed to talk to Sir Robert.

GRACE (*pleased*): Is there a bigger crowd even than yesterday, Kate?

CATHERINE: Yes, Mother, far bigger.

ARTHUR: How did it go this morning?

CATHERINE: Sir Robert finished his cross-examination of the

post-mistress. I thought he'd demolish her completely. She admitted she couldn't identify Ronnie in the Commander's office. She admitted she couldn't be sure of the time he came in. She admitted that she was called away to the telephone while he was buying his fifteen and six postal order, and that all Osborne cadets looked alike to her in their uniforms, so that it might quite easily have been another cadet who cashed the five shillings. It was a brilliant cross-examination. So gentle and quiet. He didn't bully her, or frighten her—he just coaxed her into tying herself into knots. Then when he'd finished the Attorney-General asked her again whether she was absolutely positive that the same boy that bought the fifteen and six postal order also cashed the five shilling one. She said, "Yes." She was quite, quite sure because Ronnie was such a good-looking little boy that she had specially noticed him. She hadn't said that in her examination-in-chief. I could see those twelve good men and true nodding away to each other. I believe it undid the whole of that magnificent cross-examination.

ARTHUR: If she thought him so especially good-looking, why couldn't she identify him the same evening?

CATHERINE: Don't ask me, Father. Ask the Attorney-General. I'm sure he has a beautifully reasonable answer.

DICKIE: Ronnie good-looking! What utter rot! She must be lying, that woman.

GRACE: Nonsense, Dickie! I thought he looked very well in the box yesterday, didn't you, Kate?

CATHERINE: Yes, Mother.

ARTHUR: Who else gave evidence for the other side?

CATHERINE: The Commander, the Chief Petty Officer, and one of the boys at the College.

ARTHUR: Anything very damaging?

CATHERINE: Nothing that we didn't expect. The boy showed obviously that he hated Ronnie and was torn to shreds by Sir Robert. The Commander scored, though. He's an honest man and genuinely believes Ronnie did it.

GRACE: Did you see anybody interesting in court, dear?

CATHERINE: Yes, Mother. John Watherstone.

GRACE: John? I hope you didn't speak to him, Kate.

CATHERINE: Of course I did.

GRACE: Kate, how could you! What did he say?

CATHERINE: He wished us luck.

GRACE: What impertinence! The idea of John Watherstone coming calmly up in court to wish you luck—I think it's the most disgraceful, cold-blooded——

ARTHUR: Grace—you will be late for the resumption.

GRACE: Oh, will I? Are you ready, Dickie?

DICKIE: Yes, Mother. (*He picks up his hat.*)

GRACE: You don't think that nice, grey suit of yours you paid so much money for——

ARTHUR: What time are they resuming, Kate?

CATHERINE: Two o'clock.

ARTHUR: It's twenty past two now.

GRACE: Oh, dear! We'll be terribly late. Kate—that's your fault. Arthur, you must finish your lunch——

ARTHUR: Yes, Grace.

GRACE: Promise, now.

ARTHUR: I promise.

GRACE (*to herself*): I wonder if Violet will remember to pick up those onions. Perhaps I'd better do it on the way back from the court. (To DICKIE) Now, Dickie, when you get to the front door put your head down like me, and just charge through them all.

ARTHUR: Why don't you go out by the garden?

GRACE: I wouldn't like to risk tearing this dress getting through that hedge. Come on, Dickie. I always shout: "I'm the maid and don't know nothing," so don't be surprised.

DICKIE: Right-oh, Mother.

(GRACE and DICKIE go out. There is a pause.)

ARTHUR: Are we going to lose this case, Kate?
(CATHERINE quietly shrugs her shoulders.)
It's our last chance.

CATHERINE: I know.

ARTHUR (with sudden violence): We've got to win it.
(CATHERINE does not reply.)
What does Sir Robert think?

CATHERINE: He seems very worried.

ARTHUR (thoughtfully): I wonder if you were right, Kate. I wonder if we could have had a better man.

CATHERINE: No, Father, we couldn't have had a better man.

ARTHUR: You admit that now, do you?

CATHERINE: Only that he's the best advocate in England and for some reason—prestige, I suppose—he seems genuinely anxious to win this case. I don't go back on anything else I've ever said about him.

ARTHUR: The papers said that he began to-day by telling the judge he felt ill and might have to ask for an adjournment. I trust he won't collapse——

CATHERINE: He won't. It was just another of those brilliant

tricks of his that he's always boasting about. It got him the sympathy of the court and possibly—no, I won't say that——

ARTHUR: Say it.

CATHERINE (*slowly*): Possibly provided him with an excuse if he's beaten.

ARTHUR: You don't like him, do you?

CATHERINE (*indifferently*): There's nothing in him to like or dislike, Father. I admire him.

(DESMOND *appears at the french window. He stands just inside the room.* CATHERINE *and* ARTHUR *turn and see him.*)

DESMOND: I trust you do not object to me employing this rather furtive entry. The crowds at the front door are most alarming, so I came through the garden.

ARTHUR: Come in, Desmond. Why have you left the court?

(DESMOND *puts his hat and umbrella on a chair.*)

DESMOND: My partner will be holding the fort. He is perfectly competent, I promise you——

ARTHUR: I'm glad to hear it.

DESMOND: I wonder if I might see Catherine alone. I have a matter of some urgency to communicate to her——

ARTHUR: Oh. Do you wish to hear this urgent matter, Kate?

CATHERINE: Yes, Father.

ARTHUR: Very well. I shall go and finish my lunch. (*He wheels his chair to the dining-room door.*)

DESMOND (*flying to help*): Allow me.

ARTHUR: Thank you. I can manage this vehicle without assistance. Perhaps you wouldn't mind opening the door.

(DESMOND *opens the door.* ARTHUR *goes out.* CATHERINE *sits by the table.*)

DESMOND (*closing the door and turning to* CATHERINE): I fear I should have warned you of my visit. Perhaps I have interrupted.

CATHERINE: No, Desmond. Please sit down.

(DESMOND *sits on the other side of the table.*)

DESMOND: Thank you. I'm afraid I have only a very short time. I must get back to court for the cross-examination of the Judge-Advocate.

CATHERINE: Yes, Desmond. Well?

DESMOND: I have a taxi-cab waiting at the end of the street.

CATHERINE (*smiling*): How very extravagant of you, Desmond.

DESMOND (*also smiling*): Yes. But it shows you how rushed this visit must necessarily be. The fact of the matter is— it suddenly occurred to me during the lunch adjournment that I had better see you to-day——

CATHERINE (*her thoughts far distant*): Why?

DESMOND: I have a question to put to you, Kate, which, if I had postponed putting until after the verdict, you might—who knows—have thought had been prompted by pity—if we had lost. Or—if we had won, your reply might—again who knows—have been influenced by gratitude. Do you follow me, Kate?

CATHERINE: Yes, Desmond. I think I do.

DESMOND: Ah. Then possibly you have some inkling of what the question is I have to put to you?

CATHERINE: Yes, I think I have.

DESMOND (*a trifle disconcerted*): Oh.

CATHERINE: I'm sorry, Desmond. I ought, I know, to have followed the usual practice in such cases, and told you I had no inkling whatever.

DESMOND: No, no. Your directness and honesty are two of the qualities I so much admire in you. I am glad you have guessed. It makes my task the easier——

CATHERINE (*in a matter-of-fact voice*): Will you give me a few days to think it over?

DESMOND: Of course. Of course.

CATHERINE: I need hardly tell you how grateful I am, Desmond.

DESMOND (*a trifle bewildered*): There is no need, Kate, no need at all——

CATHERINE: You mustn't keep your taxi waiting.

DESMOND (*fiercely*): Oh, bother my taxi. (*Recovering himself*) Forgive me, Kate, but you see I know very well what your feelings for me really are.

CATHERINE (*gently*): You do, Desmond?

DESMOND: Yes, Kate. I know quite well they have never amounted to much more than a sort of—well—shall we say, friendliness? A warm friendliness, I hope. Yes, I think perhaps we can definitely say, warm. But no more than that. That's true, isn't it?

CATHERINE (*quietly*): Yes, Desmond.

DESMOND: I know, I know. Of course, the thing is that even if I proved the most devoted and adoring husband that ever lived—which, I may say, if you give me the chance, I intend to be—your feelings for me would never —could never—amount to more than that. When I was younger it might, perhaps, have been a different story. When I played cricket for England——

(DESMOND *notices the faintest expression of pity that has crossed* CATHERINE'S *face*.)

(*Apologetically*) And of course, perhaps even that would not have made so much difference. Perhaps you feel I cling too much to my past athletic prowess. I feel it myself, sometimes—but the truth is I have not much else to cling to save that and my love for you. The athletic prowess is fading, I'm afraid, with the years and the stiffening of the muscles—but my love for you will never fade.

CATHERINE (*smiling*): That's very charmingly said, Desmond.

DESMOND: Don't make fun of me, Kate, please. I meant it, every word. (*He clears his throat*) However, let us take a more mundane approach and examine the facts. Fact One. You don't love me and never can. Fact Two. I love you, always have and always will. That is the situation —and it is a situation which, after most careful consideration, I am fully prepared to accept. I reached this decision some months ago, but thought at first it would be better to wait until this case, which is so much on all our minds, should be over. Then at lunch to-day I determined to anticipate the verdict to-morrow, and let you know what was in my mind at once. No matter what you feel or don't feel for me—no matter what you feel for anyone else, I want you to be my wife.

(*There is a pause.* CATHERINE *rises.*)

CATHERINE: I see. Thank you, Desmond. That makes everything much clearer.

DESMOND: There is much more that I had meant to say, but I shall put it in a letter.

CATHERINE: Yes, Desmond, do.

DESMOND: Then I may expect your answer in a few days?

CATHERINE: Yes, Desmond.

DESMOND: I must get back to court. (*He collects his hat,*

umbrella and gloves.) How did you think it went this morning?

CATHERINE: I thought the post-mistress restored the Admiralty's case with that point about Ronnie's looks——

DESMOND: Oh no, no, no. Not at all. There is still the overwhelming fact that she couldn't identify him. What a brilliant cross-examination, was it not?

CATHERINE: Brilliant.

DESMOND: He is a strange man, Sir Robert. At times, so cold and distant and—and——

CATHERINE: Fishlike.

DESMOND: Fishlike, exactly. And yet he has a real passion about this case. A real passion. I happen to know—of course this must on no account go any further—but I happen to know that he has made a very, very great personal sacrifice in order to bring it to court.

CATHERINE: Sacrifice? What? Of another brief?

DESMOND: No, no. That would be no sacrifice to him. No —he was offered—you really promise to keep this to yourself?

CATHERINE: My dear Desmond, whatever the Government offered him can't be as startling as all that; he's in the Opposition.

DESMOND: As it happens it was quite startling, and a most graceful compliment, if I may say so, to his performance as Attorney-General under the last government.

CATHERINE: What was he offered, Desmond?

DESMOND: The appointment of Lord Chief Justice. He turned it down simply in order to be able to carry on with the case of Winslow versus Rex. Strange are the ways of men, are they not? Good-bye, my dear.

CATHERINE: Good-bye, Desmond. (*She offers him her hand.*)

(DESMOND *takes it and, overcome with emotion, kisses it. He goes out quickly through the french window.* CATHERINE *looks after him, deep in thought. She has a puzzled, strained expression. It does not look as though it were* DESMOND *she was thinking of. The dining-room door opens and* ARTHUR *peeps round.*)

ARTHUR: May I come in now?

CATHERINE: Yes, Father. He's gone.

ARTHUR: I'm rather tired of being gazed at from the street, while eating my mutton, as though I were an animal at the zoo.

CATHERINE (*slowly*): I've been a fool, Father.

ARTHUR: Have you, my dear?

CATHERINE: An utter fool.

(ARTHUR *waits for her to make herself plain. She does not do so.*)

ARTHUR: In default of further information, I can only repeat, have you, my dear?

CATHERINE: There's no further information. I'm under a pledge of secrecy.

ARTHUR: Oh. What did Desmond want?

CATHERINE: To marry me.

ARTHUR: I trust the folly you were referring to wasn't your acceptance of him?

CATHERINE (*smiling*): No, Father. Would it be such folly, though?

ARTHUR: Lunacy.

CATHERINE: Oh, I don't know. He's nice and he's doing very well as a solicitor.

ARTHUR: Neither very compelling reasons for marrying him.

114

CATHERINE: Seriously, I shall have to think it over.

ARTHUR: Think it over, by all means. But decide against it.

CATHERINE: I'm nearly thirty, you know.

ARTHUR: Thirty isn't the end of life.

CATHERINE: It might be—for an unmarried woman, with not much looks.

ARTHUR: Rubbish.
(CATHERINE *shakes her head.*)
Better far to live and die an old maid than to marry Desmond.

CATHERINE: Even an old maid must eat.

(*There is a pause.*)

ARTHUR: I am leaving you and your mother everything, you know.

CATHERINE (*quietly*): Everything?

ARTHUR: There is still a little left. (*He pauses.*) Did you take my suggestion as regards your Woman's Suffrage Association?

CATHERINE: Yes, Father.

ARTHUR: You demanded a salary?

CATHERINE: I asked for one.

ARTHUR: And they're going to give it to you, I trust.

CATHERINE: Yes, Father. Two pounds a week.

ARTHUR (*angrily*): That's insulting.

CATHERINE: No. It's generous. It's all they can afford. We're not a very rich organization, you know.

ARTHUR: You'll have to think of something else.

CATHERINE: What else? Darning socks? That's about my only other accomplishment.

ARTHUR: There must be something useful you can do.

CATHERINE: You don't think the work I am doing at the W.S.A. is useful?
(ARTHUR is silent.)
You may be right. But it's the only work I'm fitted for, all the same. (She pauses) No, Father. The choice is quite simple. Either I marry Desmond and settle down into quite a comfortable and not really useless existence —or I go on for the rest of my life earning two pounds a week in the service of a hopeless cause.

ARTHUR: A hopeless cause? I've never heard you say that before.

CATHERINE: I've never felt it before.
(ARTHUR is silent.)
John's going to get married next month.

ARTHUR: Did he tell you?

CATHERINE: Yes. He was very apologetic.

ARTHUR: Apologetic!

CATHERINE: He didn't need to be. It's a girl I know slightly. She'll make him a good wife.

ARTHUR: Is he in love with her?

CATHERINE: No more than he was with me. Perhaps, even, a little less.

ARTHUR: Why is he marrying her so soon after—after——

CATHERINE: After jilting me? Because he thinks there's going to be a war. If there is his regiment will be among the first to go overseas. Besides, his father approves strongly. She's a General's daughter. Very, very suitable.

ARTHUR: Poor Kate! (He pauses. He takes her hand slowly) How I've messed up your life, haven't I?

CATHERINE: No, Father. Any messing-up that's been done has been done by me.

ARTHUR: I'm so sorry, Kate. I'm so sorry.

CATHERINE: Don't be, Father. We both knew what we were doing.

ARTHUR: Did we?

CATHERINE: I think we did.

ARTHUR: Yet our motives seem to have been different all along—yours and mine, Kate. Can we both have been right?

CATHERINE: I believe we can. I believe we have been.

ARTHUR: And yet they've always been so infernally logical, our opponents, haven't they?

CATHERINE: I'm afraid logic has never been on our side.

ARTHUR: Brute stubbornness—a selfish refusal to admit defeat. That's what your mother thinks have been our motives——

CATHERINE: Perhaps she's right. Perhaps that's all they have been.

ARTHUR: But perhaps brute stubbornness isn't such a bad quality in the face of injustice?

CATHERINE: Or in the face of tyranny. (*She pauses.*)
(*The cry of a* NEWSPAPER BOY *can be heard faintly.*)
If you could go back, Father, and choose again—would your choice be different?

ARTHUR: Perhaps.

CATHERINE: I don't think so.

ARTHUR: I don't think so, either.

CATHERINE: I still say we both knew what we were doing. And we were right to do it.

ARTHUR (*kissing the top of her head*): Dear Kate, thank you.
(*There is a silence. The* NEWSPAPER BOY *can be heard dimly shouting from the street outside.*)

You aren't going to marry Desmond, are you?

CATHERINE (*with a smile*): In the words of the Prime Minister, Father, wait and see.

(ARTHUR *squeezes her hand. The* NEWSPAPER BOY *can still be heard—now a little louder.*)

ARTHUR (*listening*): What's that boy shouting, Kate?

CATHERINE: Only—Winslow Case—latest.

ARTHUR: It didn't sound to me like " Latest."
    (CATHERINE *rises to listen at the window. Suddenly they hear it quite plainly: " Winslow Case Result! Winslow Case Result! ")*
Result?

CATHERINE: There must be some mistake.

(*There is a sudden burst of noise from the hall, which subsides as they hear the front door being slammed.* VIOLET *bursts in. She has a broad smile, and is in a fever of excitement.*)

VIOLET: Oh, sir! Oh, sir!

ARTHUR: What's happened?

VIOLET: Oh, Miss Kate, what a shame you missed it ! Just after they come back from lunch, and Mrs. Winslow she wasn't there neither nor Master Ronnie. The cheering and the shouting and the carrying-on—you never heard anything like it in all your life—and Sir Robert standing there at the table with his wig on crooked and the tears running down his face—running down his face they were and not able to speak because of the noise. Cook and me, we did a bit of crying too; we just couldn't help it—you couldn't, you know. Oh, it was lovely. We did enjoy ourselves. And then cook had her hat knocked over her eyes by the man behind who was cheering and waving his arms about something chronic and shouting about liberty—you would have laughed, Miss, to see her, she was that cross—but she didn't mind really, she was only pretending, and we kept on cheering and the judge kept on shouting, but it wasn't any good because even the jury joined in, and some of them climbed out of the box to shake hands with Sir Robert. And then outside in the street it was just the same—you couldn't move for the crowd and you'd think they'd all gone mad the way they were carrying on. Some of them were shouting, "Good old Winslow," and singing, "For he's a jolly good fellow," and cook had her hat knocked off again. Oh, it was lovely! (*To* ARTHUR) Well, sir, you must be feeling nice and pleased, now it's all over?

ARTHUR: Yes, Violet, I am.

VIOLET: That's right, I always said it would come all right in the end, didn't I?

ARTHUR: Yes, you did.

VIOLET: Two years all but one month it's been, now, since Master Ronnie came back that day. Fancy.

ARTHUR: Yes.

VIOLET: I don't mind telling you, sir, I wondered sometimes whether you and Miss Kate weren't just wasting your time carrying on the way you have. Still, you couldn't have felt that if you'd been in court to-day. (*She turns to go, then stops*) Oh, sir, Mrs. Winslow asked me to remember most particular to pick up some onions from the greengrocer, but in the excitement I'm afraid——

CATHERINE: That's all right, Violet. I think Mrs. Winslow is picking them up herself, on her way back.

VIOLET: I see, Miss. Poor madam, what a sell for her when she gets to the court and finds it's all over. Well, sir, congratulations, I'm sure.

ARTHUR: Thank you, Violet.

(VIOLET *goes out.*)

(*After a pause*) It would appear then, that we've won.

CATHERINE (*going to* ARTHUR): Yes, Father, it would appear that we've won. (*She breaks down and cries, her head on her father's lap.*)

ARTHUR (*slowly*): I would have liked to have been there.

(*There is a pause.* VIOLET *enters.*)

VIOLET (*announcing*): Sir Robert Morton.

(CATHERINE *jumps up hastily and dabs her eyes.* SIR ROBERT *comes in.* VIOLET'S *description of him in court does not seem to tally with his composed features as he walks calmly towards* ARTHUR. VIOLET *goes out.*)

SIR ROBERT: I thought you might like to hear the actual terms of the Attorney-General's statement—— (*He pulls out a scrap of paper*) So I jotted it down for you. (*He reads*) "I say now, on behalf of the Admiralty, that I accept the declaration of Ronald Arthur Winslow that he did not write the name on the postal order, that he did not take it and that he did not cash it, and that consequently he was innocent of the charge which was brought against him two years ago. I make that statement without any reservation of any description, intending it to be a complete acceptance of the boy's statements." (*He folds up the paper and hands it to* ARTHUR.)

ARTHUR: It is rather hard for me to find the words I should speak to you.

SIR ROBERT: Pray do not trouble yourself to search for them. Let us take these rather tiresome and conventional expressions of gratitude for granted, shall we? Now, on the question of damages and costs, I fear we shall find the Admiralty rather niggardly. You are likely still to be left considerably out of pocket. However, doubtless we can apply a slight spur to the First Lord's posterior in the House of Commons.

ARTHUR: Please, sir—no more trouble—I beg. Let the matter rest here. (*He indicates the piece of paper*) That is all I have ever asked for.

SIR ROBERT (*turning to* CATHERINE): A pity you were not in court, Miss Winslow. The verdict appeared to cause quite a stir.

CATHERINE: So I heard. Why did the Admiralty throw up the case?

SIR ROBERT: It was a foregone conclusion. Once the handwriting expert had been discredited—not for the first time in legal history—I knew we had a sporting chance, and no jury in the world would have convicted on the post-mistress's evidence.

CATHERINE: But this morning you seemed so depressed.

SIR ROBERT: Did I? The heat in the courtroom was very trying, you know. Perhaps I was a little fatigued——

(VIOLET *enters.*)

VIOLET (*to* ARTHUR): Oh, sir, the gentlemen at the front door say, please would you make a statement. They say they won't go away until you do.

ARTHUR: Very well, Violet. Thank you.

VIOLET: Yes, sir.

(VIOLET *goes out.*)

ARTHUR (*to* SIR ROBERT): What shall I say?

SIR ROBERT (*indifferently*): I hardly think it matters. Whatever you say will have little bearing on what they write.

ARTHUR: What shall I say, Kate?

CATHERINE: You'll think of something, Father.

(SIR ROBERT *pushes the chair towards the hall.*)

ARTHUR (*sharply*): No! I decline to meet the Press in this ridiculous chariot. (*To* CATHERINE) Get me my stick!

CATHERINE (*protestingly*): Father—you know what the doctor——

ARTHUR: Get me my stick!
(CATHERINE *goes to the piano and gets his stick for him. She and* SIR ROBERT *help him out of his chair.*)
I could say: I am happy to have lived long enough to have seen justice done to my son——

CATHERINE: It's a little gloomy, Father. You're going to live for ages yet——

(*They help him to the door.*)

ARTHUR: Am I? Wait and see. I could say: This victory is not mine. It is the people who have triumphed—as they always will triumph—over despotism. How does that strike you, sir? A trifle pretentious, perhaps.

SIR ROBERT: Perhaps. I should say it none the less. It will be very popular.

ARTHUR: Ha! Perhaps I had better say what I really feel, which is merely: Thank God we beat 'em.

(ARTHUR *goes out.* SIR ROBERT *turns abruptly to* CATHERINE.)

SIR ROBERT: Miss Winslow, might I be rude enough to ask you for a little of your excellent whisky?

CATHERINE: Of course.

(CATHERINE *goes into the dining-room.* SIR ROBERT, *left alone, droops his shoulders wearily. He subsides into a chair. When* CATHERINE *enters with the whisky he straightens his shoulders instinctively but does not rise.*)

SIR ROBERT: That is very kind. Perhaps you would forgive me not getting up? The heat in that court-room was really so infernal. (*He takes the glass from her and drains it quickly.*)

CATHERINE (*noticing his hand is trembling slightly*): Are you feeling all right, Sir Robert?

SIR ROBERT: Just a slight nervous reaction—that is all. Besides, I have not been feeling myself all day. I told the judge so this morning, if you remember, but I doubt if he believed me. He thought it was a trick. What suspicious minds people have, have they not?

CATHERINE: Yes.

SIR ROBERT (*handing her back the glass*): Thank you.

(CATHERINE *puts the glass down. She turns slowly to face* SIR ROBERT *as if nerving herself for an ordeal.*)

CATHERINE: Sir Robert, I'm afraid I have a confession and an apology to make to you.

SIR ROBERT (*sensing what is coming*): My dear young lady —I am sure the one is rash and the other superfluous. I would far rather hear neither——

CATHERINE (*with a smile*): I am afraid you must. This is probably the last time I shall see you, and it is a better penance for me to say this than to write it. I have entirely misjudged your attitude to this case, and if in doing so I have ever seemed to you either rude or ungrateful, I am sincerely and humbly sorry.

SIR ROBERT (*indifferently*): My dear Miss Winslow, you have never seemed to me either rude or ungrateful. And my attitude to this case has been the same as yours—a determination to win at all costs. Only—when you talk of gratitude—you must remember that those costs were not mine but yours.

CATHERINE: Weren't they yours also, Sir Robert?

SIR ROBERT: I beg your pardon?

CATHERINE: Haven't you, too, made a very special sacrifice for the case?

SIR ROBERT (*after a pause*): The robes of that office would not have suited me.

CATHERINE: Wouldn't they?

SIR ROBERT (*with venom*): And what is more, I fully intend to report Curry to the Law Society. (*He rises.*)

CATHERINE: Please don't. He did me a great service by telling me——

SIR ROBERT: Well, I must ask you never to divulge it to another living soul, and even to forget it yourself.

CATHERINE: I shall never divulge it. I'm afraid I can't promise to forget it myself.

SIR ROBERT: Very well! If you choose to endow an unimportant incident with a romantic significance, you are perfectly at liberty to do so. I must go. (*He offers his hand to CATHERINE.*)

CATHERINE: Why are you always at such pains to prevent people knowing the truth about you, Sir Robert?

SIR ROBERT: Am I indeed?

CATHERINE: You know you are. Why?

SIR ROBERT: Perhaps because I do not know the truth about myself.

CATHERINE: That is no answer.

SIR ROBERT: My dear Miss Winslow, are you cross-examining me?

CATHERINE: On this point, yes. Why are you so ashamed of your emotions?

SIR ROBERT: Because, as a lawyer, I must necessarily distrust them.

CATHERINE: Why?

SIR ROBERT: To fight a case on emotional grounds is the surest way of losing it. Emotions muddy the issue. Cold, clear logic—and buckets of it—should be the lawyer's only equipment.

CATHERINE: Was it cold clear logic that made you weep to-day at the verdict.

SIR ROBERT (*after a slight pause*): Your maid, I suppose, told you that? It doesn't matter. It will be in the papers to-morrow, anyway. (*Fiercely*) Very well, then, if you must have it, here it is: I wept to-day because right had been done.

CATHERINE: Not justice?

SIR ROBERT: No. Not justice. Right. It is not hard to do justice—very hard to do right. Unfortunately, while the appeal of justice is intellectual, the appeal of right appears, for some odd reason, to induce tears in court. That is my answer and my excuse. And now, may I leave the witness box?

CATHERINE: No. One last question. How can you reconcile your support of Winslow against the Crown with your political beliefs?

SIR ROBERT: Very easily. No one party has a monopoly of concern for individual liberty. On that issue all parties are united.

CATHERINE: I don't think so.

SIR ROBERT: You don't?

CATHERINE: No. Not all parties. Only some people from all parties.

SIR ROBERT: That is a wise remark. We can only hope, then, that those "some people" will always prove enough people. You would make a good advocate.

CATHERINE: Would I?

SIR ROBERT (*playfully*): Why do you not canalize your feministic impulses towards the law-courts, Miss Winslow, and abandon the lost cause of women's suffrage?

CATHERINE : Because I don't believe it *is* a lost cause.

SIR ROBERT : No? Are you going to continue to pursue it?

CATHERINE : Certainly.

SIR ROBERT : You will be wasting your time.

CATHERINE : I don't think so.

SIR ROBERT : A pity. In the House of Commons in days to come I shall make a point of looking up at the Gallery in the hope of catching a glimpse of you in that provocative hat.

(*Enter* RONNIE. *He is fifteen now, and there are distinct signs of an incipient man-about-town. He is very smartly dressed in lounge suit and bowler hat.*)

RONNIE : I say, Sir Robert, I'm most awfully sorry. I didn't know anything was going to happen.

SIR ROBERT : Where were you?

RONNIE : At the pictures.

SIR ROBERT : Pictures? What is that?

CATHERINE : Cinematograph show.

RONNIE : I'm most awfully sorry. I say—we won, didn't we?

SIR ROBERT : Yes, we won. Well, good-bye, Miss Winslow. Shall I see you in the House, then, one day? (*He offers his hand.*)

CATHERINE (*shaking his hand; with a smile*): Yes, Sir Robert. One day. But not in the Gallery. Across the floor.

SIR ROBERT (*with a faint smile*): Perhaps. Good-bye. (*He turns to go.*)

SLOW CURTAIN

Glossary: reading the text

Act 1, scene 1

1 *drawing-room* sitting room, lounge.

betoken suggest.

periodicals magazines.

the gramophone with a horn early gramophones had a horn which increased the sound that they produced.

Osborne naval cadet Ronnie is a student at the Royal Naval College at Osborne on the Isle of Wight. As such he is already considered to be a cadet in the Navy.

as though contemplating flight he is thinking about running away.

with ill-managed sang-froid he isn't able to stay composed or hide his emotions.

2 *I never did* (slang) an exclamation of surprise.

trunk storage box like a large suitcase.

tuckbox box for food.

a bit soft in the head (slang) a bit stupid.

dress clothes formal suits.

3 *the perusal* his reading of the letter.

deliberately cultured patriarchal air he has intentionally built up an appearance of a strong father whose opinions should not be questioned.

at odd variance mother and daughter seem very different.

4 *inaudible* speaking too quietly to be heard.

ethics the science that deals with morals.

Doddery old and frail.

needed the whip coming round the bend Dickie is describing the vicar's walk to the pulpit in horse-racing terms.

mods　the first examination for a Bachelor of Arts degree at Oxford University.

vac　(short for 'vacation') holiday.

5　*emanating*　coming from.

Bunny Hug/Turkey Trot/Fox Trot/Boston Glide/Kangaroo Hop　These are the names of various dance sequences for ragtime music. They were popular with the younger generation and frowned upon by the older generation at this time.

6　*obscenity*　offensive act.

going the pace　(slang) living life at a fast pace, looking for excitement.

the season　period of the year from May to July, when wealthy, upper-class young ladies (débutantes) entered fashionable London society.

a bit thick　– (slang) Dick thinks his parents are not being fair.

footling　unimportant.

7　*an air of hauteur*　assuming the look of someone above him or more important than himself.

8　*National Gallery*　art gallery in Trafalgar Square, London. Arthur is being sarcastic.

The Victoria and Albert Museum　museum in South Kensington, London.

Punch　a magazine which takes a comical look at current affairs.

simply pelting　(slang) raining very hard.

Len Rogers　a trade-union leader. This character may have been based on the MP J H Wilson who, in 1893, took the *Evening News* to court accusing them of libel against him. They had suggested that he mismanaged the union's money. Catherine admires Len Rogers for his extreme political views.

radical　person who wants the whole political system of the country to change.

suffragette　member of the Women's Social and Political Union, who campaigned for women to be given the right to vote. The extremists in the movement were prepared to go to great lengths in order to draw attention to their beliefs. See Introduction, page xiv.

9 *primed* prepared, told what to do in advance.

forbid the match it was the custom for a man wishing to marry to ask permission of his fiancée's father. The father could stop the wedding taking place if he disapproved of the man his daughter had chosen. As women had no finances of their own it was important to get the father's approval and dowry (financial settlement).

elope run away together either to marry secretly or to live as man and wife.

Byron (1788-1824) English Romantic poet, known for his stormy love affairs and therefore considered appropriate reading for people in love.

10 *New Woman* a woman who believes women should be more independent and equal to men.

dense stupid.

get under his skin (slang) get to know him well.

11 *stage whisper* loud whisper which is meant to be heard.

testily irritably.

a trifle a little.

12 *morning coat...this occasion* he is wearing the formal clothes one might wear for church or to impress Mr Winslow.

arthritis painful swelling causing stiff joints.

with a faint smile Mr Winslow is probably amused that John is trying so hard to impress him.

13 *quibble* argue over slight differences of opinion.

take the sentimental side of the project for granted Mr Winslow assumes without question that John's love for Catherine is sincere and goes on to talk of the financial exchanges involved in the marriage.

It's your duty as women were financially dependent on their husbands at this time, the father of the bride needed to be sure that his daughter would be properly provided for, and that the groom could afford to look after a wife.

the regular army John is a soldier and this work is not well paid.

subaltern John is commissioned to a junior rank (below that of captain), and therefore earns more than an ordinary soldier.

14 *Hitchey-Koo*   popular song at this time.

touch the bell   servants were called by bells which could be pressed in the main rooms of the house and which rang below stairs where the servants worked.

Westminster Bank   a British bank.

cacophonous hullabaloo   loud and terrible noise.

infernal   mild swear word: awful.

ragtime   latest dance music of the time based on American jazz.

15 *under-between maid*   an undermaid was a low-ranking female servant, a between maid being the next job on, in terms of responsibility. Violet has no definite role in the house, but appears to do everything. A richer household might have had an undermaid and a between maid.

er – other reasons   Mr Winslow perhaps doesn't wish Dickie's lack of academic success to be known about outside the family.

dowry   money and goods traditionally given by the father-in-law to his daughter's new husband.

16 *beggars can't be choosers*   Mr Winslow is using a well-known saying to suggest that he has no choice but to give this amount, and John, if he wants to marry Catherine, has no choice but to accept.

17 *a swell*   (slang) well-dressed person.

the Knuts   (slang) a fashionably-dressed man pronounced 'nuts'.

coyly   pretending to be shy.

18 *neatly turned*   carefully worded.

Poole's   fashionable tailors in London.

monocle   an eyeglass worn in only one eye.

19 *bedraggled and woe-begone*   untidy and miserable.

be a little more explicit   explain what you mean exactly.

What on earth   expression of astonishment.

20 *Petty Officer*   an officer in the Navy. As Osborne was a naval school, students were used to being disciplined by officers in the Navy. See note to page 1.

21 *sacked* (slang) expelled.

22 *pinch* (slang) steal.

pneumonia severe illness affecting the lungs.

23 *keep* cave (slang) watch to see if anyone is coming.

24 *the Service* Ronnie is already part of the Navy as he goes to naval school.

to clear himself prove his innocence.

25 *family solicitor* the person whom the Winslows usually employed to deal with any legal matters.

family joke Desmond's love for Kate was known of by the family and not taken seriously.

gone to seed no longer fit.

just absconded with his firm's petty cash he seems guiltily nervous, as if he has committed a petty crime.

Dead on time (slang) exactly on time.

26 *Capital* (slang) jolly good.

hearing it like that – from Violet in the hall another indication that Violet doesn't behave correctly as a servant. See note to page 15.

Fancy mild expression of surprise.

27 *Middlesex* top-class county cricket team based at Lord's Cricket Ground in London.

Hat trick this is an expression used in cricket when three batsmen in a row are got out, by one bowler. The fact that Desmond achieved this shows that he was a fine cricketer in his youth.

the Players professional cricketers were known as 'Players' and amateurs were 'Gentlemen'.

28 *overs* an over is six balls bowled.

maidens overs in which the batsmen don't score any runs.

wicket a batsman's innings. In making all these references, Desmond is showing off about his greatest match in cricket, 'Curry's match', as it became known, because of his fine performance.

protuberant sticking out. His paunch is a sign of the fact that he is no longer fit to play the same standard of cricket.

Madeira fortified wine named after the island where it is produced; drunk before a meal, like sherry.

29 *Happy pair* traditional description of a couple who have become engaged.

A forlorn quest it would be impossible to say anything new about engaged couples as they are so common. Grace thinks Arthur is suggesting that Desmond could say nothing new because he has no imagination.

Voltaire (1694-1778) French writer, known for his originality.

spliced up (slang) term for a couple getting married.

withdrawn to stud the term given to a horse that is used for breeding once it is too old to race.

Good egg! (slang) jolly good!

We defy augury We're not scared of superstition (augury being the Roman art of fortune-telling). John is also quoting from *Hamlet* (Act 5, scene 2) by William Shakespeare. The statement is ironic, as later events suggest that neither he, nor Hamlet, should have dismissed 'augury' so lightly.

30 *allayed* diminished, set aside.

on the 7th instant on the 7th of this month.

the gong percussion instrument used to inform the household that a meal is ready.

33 *decant* pour wine from the bottle into a decanter.

claret red wine of Bordeaux.

an appreciable pause pause that is long enough to be noticed.

the threshold he is standing in the doorway, suggesting his nervousness of coming in.

35 *trunk call* long-distance telephone call made through the operator.

---

1 What information have you gained about Ronnie's expulsion from school?

2 In what different ways do the characters react to the news of Ronnie's expulsion?

3 What impression do you have of Mr Winslow? What do you expect him to say on the phone?

4 What do you think will happen next?

Act 1, scene 2

35 *Alexander's Ragtime Band*   popular song at the time.

essays a little pas seul   he dances a little on his own.

36 *Soft needle and an old sweater down the horn*   ways of reducing the sound produced by the gramophone.

What's the verdict   Dickie is referring to his father's consultation as if it were a trial, suggesting that the doctor has the power to free or condemn Mr Winslow.

Fat chance   (slang) there is little or no chance.

a treat   (slang) very nice.

done up   (slang) altered to match the latest fashion and to appear new. This suggests that the family is already poorer than they had been.

Daly's   a music hall in London.

the Cri   (short for The 'Criterion') a London restaurant.

In your new feminine world   he refers to the world that would come about if the feminist movement were successful.

37 *to chain themselves to Mr Asquith*   Dickie creates a comical image of women chained to the Prime Minister of the time. He is alluding to the demonstrations made by the extremists in the suffrage movement, who chained themselves to civic buildings in order to draw attention to their beliefs.

you can jolly well call on me   Dickie's light-hearted comment that he would support women's suffrage if it led to women paying their way, highlights the fact that men at this time always paid for their female companions.

this side of Doomsday   (slang) the day on which the world will cease to exist. Dickie suggests that if he asked Edwina for money he would never see her again as it was considered improper for women to pay for an evening out.

salver   small tray used by servants to bring in letters and similar.

The Star   London evening newspaper.

Democrat   rather than giving a name, the writer of the letter remains anonymous, whilst still expressing her/his political views.

soulless oligarchy   an elite and uncaring ruling power.

37-8 *despotism of Whitehall*   tyrannical rule by central government. Whitehall is near to the Houses of Parliament, and many government officials work there.

The Englishman's home…his castle   saying meaning that a person has the right to manage his own affairs. The writer of the letter uses it to suggest that a person should have the right to individual expression against those in power. See note to Democrat above.

38 *Libertatis Amator*   (Latin) lover of freedom.

present troubles in the Balkans   a political unrest in the Balkan States led to the outbreak of the First World War in 1914.

a certain major European Power   the writer is referring to Germany.

the Judge Advocate of the Fleet   legal adviser to the Crown on all naval matters.

This correspondence must now cease   an editor would close a subject (meaning he would no longer print letters written on a topic) once he felt there was no new angle to consider. The fact that he closes this correspondence indicates that there have already been several letters on the topic.

old man   slang term for father.

39 *Feminism*   the belief that women should be equal to men.

happy date   common phrase for the wedding day.

but not too emphatically   Catherine is showing in her smile that she is not completely happy; there is a lack of certainty in the expression.

40 *half-witted*   lacking intelligence.

Ramsay MacDonald   first Labour Prime Minister in 1924.

41 *a guinea*   a gold coin worth twenty-one shillings. The coin itself was no longer being used in 1913 but the amount was quoted for professional fees.

impedimenta   nuisances.

in deference to his father's presence   Dickie is only working because his father is in the room to see him. He wishes to impress him.

libellous   a legal term for writings which could destroy someone's reputation.

merely base   cruel and unpleasant.

Dickie is elaborately industrious   he is making a show of working.

42 *your bookmaker friends...*   Mr Winslow does not think it likely that his son will gain a degree and he speaks in terms of 'odds' and 'bets' as this is the language Dickie understands from his own activities in betting on horses. A bookmaker is someone who organises betting.

evens   an even chance in betting terms. If a bet was placed you would win or lose the same amount.

takers   people prepared to gamble.

seven to four against   the bookmaker would pay out seven pounds for every four pounds in a bet if Dickie got a degree.

a bit steeper   Dickie is not likely to become a civil servant if he does not get a degree.

gamble two hundred pounds a year   this is the fee Mr Winslow is paying for Dickie's education at Oxford.

an outside chance   a horse which is not likely to win.

43 *work like a black*   at this time black people were thought of in England as inferior people who were expected to work for little or no reward. Dickie is using the term to show he is prepared to make great sacrifices in order to stay on at Oxford.

hoping to brief   to employ him as a lawyer.

forlornly   he feels neglected and wretched.

44 *sovereign*   gold coin worth one pound. It is no longer in circulation.

a little spot of something   (slang) alcoholic drink.

fortitude   strength, courage.

Oh, rot   (slang) Nonsense!

Daily News   popular daily newspaper at that time.

45 *gushing*   insincerely expressing admiration.

simpering   making a foolish unnatural smile.

winces visibly   he makes an involuntary move in his expression which the audience can see and shows he is uncomfortable with her choice of words.

line of country   (slang) area of interest.

46 *implying*   suggesting in roundabout terms.

advocate   defence lawyer.

47 *Court Martial*   a military trial where the accused would be allowed to have legal representation, and all the evidence would have to be considered.

civil trial   normal public trial.

questions in the House   MPs can ask government ministers questions publicly in the House of Commons. The subjects for questions may come from people in their constituency.

independent enquiry   the matter would be looked into by people outside the Admiralty – the actual enquiry clearly does not live up to its name.

Judge Advocate of the Fleet   see note to page 38.

Fancy   see note to page 26.

forger   someone who fakes someone else's signature for illegal purposes.

48 *boisterously*   noisily, full of energy.

absolutely tophole   (slang) feeling very happy, in excellent health.

sibilant   sounding like 'sh'.

listless   uninterested.

apparatus   equipment such as camera and tripod.

49 *Barker's*   large department store in Kensington, London.

50 *perturbation*   worry.

Divinity   Religious instruction.

51 *chattering shrilly*   talking constantly in a high-pitched voice.

to the purpose   of value, to the point.

52 *witches' brew*   Mr Winslow does not think the ointment will be of any use.

Mme Dupont   Mrs Winslow refers to the seamstress who has altered the dress. (See note to page 36.)

Photo inset   a photograph in a newspaper.

marriage settlement   money Mr Winslow has promised to give to John when he marries Catherine.

53 *roused*   talking with feeling.

monopoly   the complete control of a particular area of business.

Tory paper   a newspaper whose editorials are written with a bias in favour of the Conservative party.

Labour leader   person who is prominent in the Labour Party.

54 *the boot is entirely on the other foot*   the situation is reversed.

women's suffrage   see note to page 8.

Trades Disputes Bill   an Act of Parliament which made it illegal for an employer to sue a trade union for money lost during union action.

in the words of the Prime Minister let us wait and see!   the Prime Minister used the phrase 'We had better wait and see' in speeches in 1910 and his opponents used it against him.

55 *jilted*   given up as a companion.

scratched from the Oxford Stakes   Dickie is using a term used in horse racing to describe his withdrawal from University.

in the wind   being talked about, likely to happen.

plumb   (slang) completely.

nabbed   (slang) caught.

blighter   (slang) nuisance.

56 *cadaverous*   thin, very pale.

a fop   someone who is over-concerned with being fashionable.

supercilious   superior, haughty.

chambers   barristers' offices.

57 *Some people find it shocking*   some thought it was unsuitable for a 'lady' to be seen smoking in public.

Devonshire House   until 1924 the London home of the Duke of Devonshire. The house was an important political and social centre.

58 *a collusive action*   legal term describing the secret agreement of two parties to stand against a third party and take the latter to court.

forensic triumphs   impressive cross-examinations of evidence on which legal cases were won.

Len Rogers   see note to page 8.

embezzlement   taking, for personal use, goods or money which you only have the right to 'spend' as part of your work.

59 *It's the politeness of princes*   she is misquoting: 'Punctuality is the politeness of kings'.

60 *Petition of Right*   as the Navy belonged to the King or Queen, taking the Admiralty to court would be like accusing royalty of doing wrong, which in legal terms was not possible. The only way round this was for an individual to ask the King or Queen, via Parliament, to be allowed to bring the matter to trial. If this request was refused the issue had to be discussed in the House of Commons. Here a vote could be taken or the Government might change its mind in order to avoid political embarrassment.

Attorney-General   an MP who acts as the King or Queen's lawyer.

languidly   weakly.

Eton suit   formal uniform worn by pupils at Eton College but adopted by other public schools.

spick and span   carefully dressed, clean.

61 *prep.*   time given to complete homework.

Chief Petty Officer   non-commissioned officer in the Navy.

62 *incentive*   reason.

P.O.   Petty Officer (See note above.)

63 *Commander*   senior commissioned officer in the Navy. The head teacher at Ronnie's naval college.

sanitorium   room in which boarding-school children are cared for when they are sick.

furtively   avoiding being noticed.

64 *that particular form*   the specific way in which the signature is written.

66 *impertinent*   rude.

67 *rattled*   (slang) upset.

68 *C.O.*   Commanding Officer. (See note to page 63.)

with searing sarcasm   a tone of unkind scorn.

69 *rifling*   searching through with the intention of stealing anything valuable.

70 *Judge Advocate*   the usual prosecutor for the Crown at a court martial (see note to page 38).

venom   hatred.

71 *hysterically*   in an uncontrolled manner.

indignantly   showing justifiable anger.

---

1   What new events have taken place between this and the first scene of the play?

2   In what ways has the family's lifestyle altered since Ronnie was expelled?

3   What impression do you get of Sir Robert Morton in this scene?

4   What do you expect will happen in the next scene?

Act 2, scene 1

73 *histrionic hyperbole*   the words are over-stated because of over excitement.

Right Honourable and learned gentleman opposite   Sir Robert is being addressed in the manner which MPs adopt in parliamentary debates.

First Lord   official title of the government minister responsible for the Navy.

rough passage   a difficult time.

74 *oblivious*   unaware of what's going on.

demurrer   a legal plea where the action of the court is stopped by one side stating that they do not feel that the evidence being presented by the other side is relevant to the case.

menaced...by the new despotism of bureaucracy   threatened by the laws enforced by the government.

resonant   ringing, musical.

75 *precedents*   decisions that could be used to justify similar actions in the future.

private rights...public good   individual rights may need to be given up so that everyone may benefit.

Charles 1...ship money   unpopular ancient tax often referred to when individual freedom was thought to be threatened by a central power.

dead tired   (slang) completely exhausted.

76 *m'm*   abbreviation for madam, often used by servants.

grasp the nettle   raise a difficult topic for discussion.

faced the situation squarely   faced up to what had to be done.

77 *common or garden*   (slang) ordinary.

thrown all that overboard   (slang) not considered, sacrificed too freely.

publish   tell everyone about.

weigh the cost   consider the losses and make decisions in the light of them.

78 *heroics*   behaviour which appears brave but means nothing.

The Winslow boy is bad enough   it doesn't matter whether he did or didn't do it; being known as the boy in the Winslow case is harmful in itself, with everyone talking about him.

gout   disease which makes the joints, especially in the feet and toes, swell and give pain.

79 *salver*   see note to page 37.

80 *fine old rumpus*   (slang) a real uproar.

wonders will never cease   (slang) things that occur continue to surprise.

81 *An Honourable Member*   Member of Parliament (see note to page 73).

Dartmouth   the South Devon Royal Naval College.

iniquitous   unjust.

a division   a vote in a parliamentary debate.

motion   the discussion topic in a parliamentary debate.

To reduce...by a hundred pounds   if a government minister falls short of performing his duties it is customary for MPs in the opposition to ask for the minister's salary to be cut.

82 *fishy*   (slang) distant, unfeeling. Perhaps dishonest.

83 *staunch*   firm, trusty.

a nice popular stick to beat the Government with   because it is popular it can be used to attack the government.

a fish   (slang) someone who has no feeling (see note to page 82).

supercilious   superior, or thinking himself superior.

forestalled   beaten, arrived before.

gallery   place from which members of the public can listen to debates in the House of Commons.

gallantly   politely attentive to a lady; here Sir Robert is teasing Catherine.

84 casus belli   (Latin) the cause of war; here referring to Ronnie, who is at the centre of the problem.

dormant   sleeping.

technical secret   Catherine is asking Sir Robert to tell her a trade secret of his art of cross-examination.

loophole   way of escaping.

85 *put out*   (slang).

Director of Public Prosecutions   the official who sets up a court case for the Attorney-General.

86 *amiss*   wrong.

vivacity   liveliness, vitality.

87 *Balderdash!*   (slang) Nonsense!

unparliamentary expression   strong or abusive language is not allowed in Parliament.

laughing-stock   source of the joke, something to be laughed at, the object of ridicule.

88 *undertaking*   promise.

ultimatum   last statement of conditions that must be met.

of age   over twenty-one, therefore he does not need his father's permission to marry. (The current age for becoming legally an adult is eighteen.)

bravado   confidence in a difficult situation.

Negligible   so small as to be unimportant.

89 *deprecating*   he is embarrased by Mr Winslow's praise.

ventilation   circulation of fresh air.

hot air   (slang) irrelevant discussion.

political persuasion   political beliefs.

to have the best of both worlds   to dress in a feminine way whilst wishing to be considered as men.

militant   fighting aggressively for a belief.

90 *propagate*   increase support for.

Women's Suffrage Association   see note to page 8.

lucrative   financially rewarding, profitable.

convictions   beliefs.

91 *shamming*   pretending.

92 *blackmail*   threatening someone in order to change their behaviour.

in the soup   (slang) in real trouble.

two can live as cheaply as one   a saying which implies that it is as cheap to provide for two people when they are married as it is to provide for one who is not.

93 *five bob*   (slang) five shillings.

diehard   person who refuses to update his/her old-fashioned attitudes.

94 *European war*   John is speaking of the threat of the First World War, which began in 1914.

coal strike   the coal miners' strike of 1912.

civil war in Ireland   John is speaking of the disagreements in Ireland between those who wanted Home Rule and those who wished to continue to be ruled by England.

bally   (slang) a mild version of the swear word 'bloody'.

95 *a bit steep*   (slang) an exaggeration.

the mess   room used for dining and social activities in the armed forces.

in front of the House of Lords   the Lords can act as a supreme court of law.

Adjutant's bath   this would be an old portable bath and its theft would represent a very petty crime.

the Alhambra   music hall.

quod   (slang) prison.

sued   took him to court.

97 *scathing denunciations*   bitterly cruel speech showing strong disapproval.

all parts   from both sides of the House of Commons. Government and opposition MPs disagreed with the First Lord's words.

Winslow versus Rex   legal way of naming a lawsuit.

---

1 What new developments occur in the case during this scene?

2 What are Grace's arguments against the continuation of the case? Do you think she is right in her opinions?

3 How has the case altered Catherine's and John's opinions of each other?

4 What type of relationship has formed between Catherine and Sir Robert Morton?

5 How do you expect the case to end? How do you expect the play to end?

Act 2, scene 2

99 *Daily Mail*   popular daily newspaper.

Reading   county town of Berkshire.

fretwork   patterns cut in thin wood; a boy's hobby at the time.

100 *Reading's Savile Row*   Savile Row in London was considered to be the best place for a gentleman to buy a suit. Dickie had bought his suit from the best tailors in Reading.

Off the peg   made to a standard size, not made to measure (therefore cheaper).

101 *people being turned out*   removed from the court.

hammer and tongs   (slang) with all their energy.

demurrers   see note to page 74.

prerogatives   rights in law.

102 *ludicrous form of propulsion*   Mr Winslow feels ridiculous using a wheelchair.

Good egg!   see note to page 29.

decent old stick   (slang) a kind but uninteresting person.

the old baa-lamb   (slang) the nickname Dickie had given to Mr Lamb.

lost his shirt   (slang) lost a great deal of money at the races.

bookmaking establishment   betting shop.

territorials   British Army reserve soldiers.

a bit of a scrap   (slang) a minor fight.

103 *This isn't a cricket match*   because Mrs Winslow uses the word 'interval' she makes the court proceedings sound like a performance.

a matinee at the Gaiety   afternoon performance at a theatre. Mr Winslow is pointing out that his wife is more suitably dressed for a theatre visit than for her son's trial.

get-up   (slang) choice of clothes.

Mme Dupont   Grace and Catherine's seamstress.

under sentence   Dickie uses legal words to describe the fact that Violet may lose her job.

104 *a nursing home*   private hospital.

105 *pick up the pieces*   (slang) sort things out when they've gone wrong.

in at the death   (slang) Catherine refers to the trial as if it were a fight – like gladiators in the Roman arena when one of the fighters had to die to bring about the end of the contest. She also implies that they are to be the losers in the trial.

simultaneously cause a mutiny...jubilation in Berlin   Catherine is describing the Attorney-General's suggestion that if Ronnie won the case it would make Britain lose confidence and look foolish abroad.

106 *tying herself into knots*   (slang) getting confused in what she was saying, contradicting herself.

examination-in-chief   the evidence the post-mistress gave when she was first called.

twelve good men and true   at this time the twelve people on the jury would all have been men.

107 *What impertinence!*   How rude! She suggests he is intrusive and that he is behaving unacceptably.

the resumption   the re-opening of the case after lunch.

108 *don't know nothing* Mrs Winslow thinks the maid might use an ungrammatical expression like this.

109 *furtive* stealthy, secretive.

holding the fort (slang) Desmond's partner is taking care of the affairs of the court while Desmond visits Catherine.

110 *inkling* idea.

a trifle disconcerted a little put off, disturbed.

111 *bother* (slang) meaning: it doesn't matter about my taxi!

112 *athletic prowess* abilities in sport.

mundane straightforward, ordinary, down-to-earth.

113 *he's in the Opposition* the party opposing the government (and therefore Sir Robert is unlikely to have been offered an important position).

under the last government we are told that Sir Robert served in the Conservative Government which was overwhelmingly out-voted by the Liberal Party in the General Election of 1906.

Lord Chief Justice a position of great power in the legal profession. If Sir Robert had taken the appointment he couldn't have continued as a barrister.

114 *In default of further information* without you telling me more.

pledge promise.

folly foolishness.

Lunacy madness.

115 *an old maid* an unmarried older woman.

116 *W.S.A.* Women's Suffrage Association.

a hopeless cause an aim which will never be achieved.

117 *infernally* (slang) annoyingly.

opponents people who take up a position against you. In this case the Admiralty and those who support them.

tyranny where those who govern have absolute power and use it cruelly.

118 *In the words of the Prime Minister* see note to page 54.

119 *something chronic*   (slang) a great deal.

For he's a jolly good fellow   popular song, once used to drink somebody's health, but now often sung by crowds to celebrate a person's special achievement.

what a sell   (slang) what a pity.

120 *does not seem to tally*   does not match, he is quite different.

damages and costs   the money given after a court case by the party who loses, to the party who wins.

niggardly   grudging in giving money, stingy.

out of pocket   less well off.

121 *apply a slight spur to the First Lord's posterior*   try and speed up the Admiralty.

sporting chance   (slang) good chance of winning.

122 *despotism*   tyranny, the abuse of power.

a trifle pretentious   over-assuming, claiming too much.

123 *rash*   hasty, lacking caution.

superfluous   unnecessary, more than enough.

penance   making a sacrifice in order to punish herself.

The robes of that office   the Lord Chief Justices clothes. He means that he would have felt uncomfortable in that job.

124 *the Law Society*   the body governing solicitors' behaviour.

to endow an unimportant incident with a romantic significance   he suggests she is creating an idealised picture of his turning down the job; he suggests it was, in fact, no sacrifice to him.

muddy the issue   cause confusion.

125 *No one party...individual liberty*   all parties are capable of doing right regardless of their differing political beliefs.

canalize your feministic impulses   Sir Robert is suggesting that Catherine should give up fighting for women's rights and instead fight for her clients in court, as a barrister.

126 *Gallery*   see note to page 83.

incipient man-about-town Ronnie is beginning to look fashionable and grown-up.

the pictures...Cinematograph silent films were just beginning at this time.

But not in the Gallery. Across the floor Catherine believes that one day she will be able to participate in government as an MP, not just be present as a spectator. She would be in the party opposing the Conservatives and therefore sit opposite Sir Robert in the House of Commons.

---

1 How has the case proceeded in this scene?
2 Why did Desmond visit the house before the case closed?
3 In what ways has Dickie changed since the first act of the play?

■ Study programme

What is the play about?

☐ Look at each of the following statements about the play and decide which you feel are the most important. Place them in order of importance. There is no *right* order but you should be able to back up your decisions with your opinions.

The play is about:

1 the guilt or innocence of Ronnie Winslow;
2 the political unrest of the period before the First World War;
3 the relationship between parents and children;
4 the rights of the individual against the rights of the group;
5 the relationship between men and women;
6 issues of self-sacrifice;
7 the rights of children;
8 the importance of money;
9 the triumph of right over wrong.

☐ Having decided on an order of importance, study each of the following quotations from the play, and link each of them to one or more of the statements above. You will find it useful to look at the context of the words in the scene.

1   GRACE   (sighing) *I don't think you modern girls have the feelings our generation did. It's this New Woman attitude.*

       CATHERINE   (rising and facing Grace) *Very well, Mother. I love John in every way that a woman can love a man, and far, far more than he loves me. Does that satisfy you?*

                                          (Act 1, scene 1, page 10)

149

2   ARTHUR   *I propose to settle on her one sixth of my total capital – which worked out to the final fraction is exactly eight hundred and thirty-three pounds six and eight pence. But let us deal in round figures and say eight hundred and fifty pounds.*

        JOHN   *I call that very generous, sir.*

      ARTHUR   *Not as generous as I would have liked, I'm afraid. However – as my wife would say – beggars can't be choosers.*

                                                     (Act 1, scene 1, pages 15-16)

3   DICKIE   *…Believe me, old chap, pinching's nothing. Nothing at all…*

                                                       (Act 1, scene 1, page 22)

4   RONNIE   (reluctantly) *I was hiding.*

      ARTHUR   *From me?*

                (RONNIE nods.)

                Do you remember once, you promised me that if ever you were in trouble of any sort you would come to me first?

      RONNIE   *Yes, father*

      ARTHUR   *Why didn't you come to me now? Why did you have to go and hide in the garden?*

      RONNIE   *I don't know, Father.*

      ARTHUR   *Are you so frightened of me?*

                                                       (Act 1, scene 1, page 34)

5   GRACE   *…You talk about sacrificing everything for him; but when he's grown up he won't thank you for it, Arthur – even though you've given your life to – publish his innocence as you call it.* (ARTHUR makes an impatient gesture.)
Yes, Arthur – your life. You talk gaily about arthritis and a touch of gout and old age and the rest of it, but you know as well as any of the doctors what really is the matter with you. (Nearly in tears) *You're destroying yourself, Arthur, and me and your family besides – and for what I'd like to know? I've asked you and Kate to tell me a hundred times – but you never can. For what, Arthur?*

                                                       (Act 2, scene 1, page 78)

6   JOHN   (reasonably) *Well now, look. There's a European war blowing up, there's a coal strike on, there's a fair chance of civil war in Ireland, and there's a hundred and one other things on the horizon at the moment that I think you genuinely could call important. And yet, with all that on its mind, the House of Commons takes a whole day to discuss him –* (pointing to Ronnie) *and his bally postal order. Surely you must see that's a little out of proportion –* (He pauses.)

      CATHERINE   (with some spirit) *All I know is, John, that if ever the time comes when the House of Commons has so much on its mind that it can't find time to discuss a Ronnie Winslow and his bally postal order, this country will be a far poorer place than it is now.*

                                    (Act 2, scene 1, pages 94-5)

7   DESMOND   *…However, let us take a more mundane approach and examine the facts. Fact One. You don't love me and never can. Fact Two. I love you, always have and always will. That is the situation – and it is a situation which, after most careful consideration, I am fully prepared to accept. I reached this decision some months ago, but thought at first it would be better to wait until this case, which is so much on all our minds, should be over. Then at lunch to-day I determined to anticipate the verdict to-morrow, and let you know what was in my mind at once. No matter what you feel or don't feel for me – no matter what you feel for anyone else, I want you to be my wife.*

                                    (Act 2, scene 2, page 112)

8   ARTHUR   *Yet our motives seem to have been different all along – yours and mine, Kate. Can we both have been right?*

      CATHERINE   *I believe we can. I believe we have been.*

      ARTHUR   *And yet they've always been so infernally logical, our opponents, haven't they?*

      CATHERINE   *I'm afraid logic has never been on our side.*

      ARTHUR   *Brute stubbornness – a selfish refusal to admit defeat. That's what your mother thinks have been our motives –*

      CATHERINE   *Perhaps she's right. Perhaps that's all they have been.*

ARTHUR   *But perhaps brute stubbornness isn't such a bad quality in the face of injustice?*
CATHERINE   *Or in the face of tyranny.*

(Act 2, scene 2, page 117)

9   SIR ROBERT   *...I wept to-day because right had been done.*
CATHERINE   *Not justice?*
SIR ROBERT   *No. Not justice. Right. It is not hard to do justice – very hard to do right. Unfortunately, while the appeal of justice is intellectual, the appeal of right appears, for some odd reason, to induce tears in court.*

(Act 2, scene 2, page 125)

Have your attitudes towards the earlier statements changed at all? If necessary change the order you decided on in the first task.

③ Now look again at the statements on page 151 and take the three statements that you consider to be the most important. Work with a partner to find scenes in the play which back up your opinion. You can write down appropriate short quotations or paraphrase individual episodes.

Use the information you have gained to complete the following tasks.

④ Present your view in a class debate.

⑤ Write a letter between any two characters in which one justifies her/his behaviour in the play in terms of one or more of the statements.

⑥ Write an argumentative essay explaining why your three statements are the most important. In this you should also mention the other statements you could have chosen, and indicate why you did not find them appropriate.

⑦ Working in a group of three carry out a role-play in which two 'critics' with different opinions are interviewed by a person from the media in order to debate their opposing points of view.

The characters

The characters are obviously an important part of the play, but are there any characters that could be left out? Imagine that you are the playwright, and that a director staging a current production of *The Winslow Boy* has asked you to remove one character for financial reasons. You must decide which character should go.

▣ By looking at the text, get to know the characters well.

- Look at the cast list for the play and make sure you know which characters are which.

- Study the stage directions describing each character before they appear, so that you have a clear image of each one.

- Read through the following quotations. Each excerpt is spoken by one person in the play. Identify each speaker.

1   *Oh, is that all finally spliced up now? Kate definitely being withdrawn to stud? Good egg!*

(Act 1, scene 1)

2   *Answer me, someone! Is the boy very ill? Why must I be kept in the dark like this? Surely I have the right to know. If he's ill I must be with him –*

(Act 1, scene 1)

3   *From school? How interesting. So you got a school to take him? I mean, they didn't mind the unpleasantness?*

(Act 1, scene 2)

4   *I say, do you know how long the train took? A hundred and twenty-three miles in two hours and fifty-two minutes.*

(Act 1, scene 2)

5   *I'm afraid he can only spare us a very few minutes of his most valuable time this evening. Of course, it's a long way for him to come – so far from his chambers – and very good of him to do it, too, if I may say so...*

(Act 1, scene 2)

6   *I suggest that in continuing to deny your guilt you are causing great hardship to your own family, and considerable annoyance to high and important persons in this country...*

(Act 1, scene 2)

7   *He's perfectly happy, at a good school, doing very well. No one need ever
have known about Osborne, if you hadn't gone and shouted it out to the
whole world. As it is, whatever happens now, he'll go through the rest of his
life as the boy in that Winslow case – the boy who stole that postal order...*

(Act 2, scene 1)

8   *...An Honourable Member described that this evening as a piteous little
figure, crying aloud to humanity for justice and redress. I wish he could see
him now.*

(Act 2, scene 1)

9   *Don't you believe it. Two can live as cheaply as two, and that's all there is to
it.*

(Act 2, scene 1)

10 *I don't mind telling you, sir, I wondered sometimes whether you and Miss
Kate weren't just wasting your time carrying on the way you have. Still you
couldn't have felt that if you'd been in court to-day.*

(Act 2, scene 2)

How did you identify each character?

2   Working in a small group consider each character with regard to the
following questions:

- Is the character directly involved in the plot of the play?
- Does the character cause things to happen in the play?
- Is the character made 'real' in the play or is she or he more like a
cardboard cut-out?
- Does the character interest you; do you enjoy listening to her or his
words?
- Does the character inform other characters (and the audience) of
events going on outside the house?
- Does the character give other characters (and the audience)
information of events which have taken place before the scene?
- Does the character act as a 'sounding board' for information, or for
opinions which are important to the play?
- Does the character represent a viewpoint or a group in society which
is relevant to the action of the play?

3️⃣ Now decide which character you could most happily lose from the script, bearing in mind your responses to the questions above. Choose as well the character you would least like to lose. For both characters chosen write down as many reasons as you can for losing or keeping them.

Use the ideas you have collected to complete the following tasks.

4️⃣ Write a description of the character you consider to be the most important which could be used as an aid to an actor who is going to play the part but has only read through the script once. Explain her or his importance to the play, and the role she or he plays in it.

5️⃣ Write a letter from the playwright to the director, explaining which character you've chosen to drop, and giving your reasons why. Bear in mind the fact that Rattigan would probably have been loathe to drop any of his characters.

6️⃣ Write a letter to *The Times* written by the character you have dropped from the production, giving her or his reasons why she or he feels this treatment to have been wrong.

7️⃣ Learn one of the speeches, or a selection of lines, spoken by your favourite character. Begin by reading them through, making sure you know their meaning, and refreshing yourself as to the context in which they appear. Pay attention to the tone of voice you think you should use and which words you feel should be emphasised. Think about the actions the character may be making as they speak the lines. Act the lines before a group, explaining beforehand how they fit in to a particular scene and why you have chosen them.

Work with a partner or small group if you want to act out a dialogue.

Further ideas

8️⃣ Throughout the play similarities are drawn between Catherine and Sir Robert. For instance, they are both accused of hiding their emotions. Discuss in what ways their characters are similar and different.

⑨ *Violet is the only member of the working class shown in the play. Her opinions give us insight into the common person's view of the case.* Explain this view.

⑩ The doctor and the cook are two characters who are mentioned but never actually appear. What might their lives be like?

    (a) Write the doctor's medical log book for one day which includes information about Arthur Winslow and the other patients he has seen.

    (b) Write a letter which the cook has sent to her mother to tell her about her job and the events in the household.

The events of the play

☐ Complete a flow diagram of the main events of the play. You will need to assess which are the major and which are the minor events. Begin by sorting out the major from the minor events in the list below.

- Ronnie is expelled from Osborne.
- The family discuss the vicar's sermon.
- The family drink a toast to Kate and John's engagement.
- Dickie is told he has to leave Oxford.
- Arthur tells Miss Barnes about the events of the past months.
- Grace and Miss Barnes discuss the new material used in the curtains.
- Sir Robert Morton accepts the Winslow case.
- Grace and Arthur discuss sacking Violet.
- John and Kate's engagement is broken off.

Now looking at the whole play try to decide on ten main events within it.

Compare your list with a partner and combine your ideas to find fifteen main events.

Now combine with a small group and agree on twenty main events and use these to complete your flow diagram.

Events which we do not see

Many of the events of the play take place outside the Winslows' living room. Choose from the following assignments to complete on your own or in a group.

1. Act out the events which you believe took place on 7 July, at the Royal Naval College at Osborne, when Ronnie was said to have stolen the postal order.

2. Write the article which Miss Barnes submits to the newspaper after her interview with Arthur Winslow.

3. Work with a group to script and act out one of the scenes of the trial. You could choose the cross-examination of the post-mistress or Ronnie's stand in the witness box.

4. Conduct a role-play between John and Colonel Watherstone as they discuss the contents of the letter the colonel intends to send to Arthur Winslow.

5. Script and act out one of the conversations between Violet and Cook as they discuss the latest events of the case, or the most recent letters in *The Star*.

6. Dickie takes the manager of his bank for a day at the races where he *loses his shirt* in the betting. Write Mr Lamb's diary entry for the day in which he comments on the events that took place and notes his impressions of Dickie.

7. Write a column in a national newspaper which may have been written by one of the press who have been 'camped outside' the Winslows' door.

8. A number of Admiralty officials discuss the case and the effect it has had on their public credibility. Carry out the meeting in a role-play.

What happens before and after the play?

In the play we are given a strong sense that life went on before, and will continue after, the events which we have seen taking place in the space of two years. Drawing on the information you have of the characters, their beliefs and actions in the play, complete the following tasks.

1 Write a school report of Dickie's progress when he was fourteen.

2 Desmond Curry used to play for Middlesex and England. Write the commentary of one of his most famous cricket matches.

3 Violet has been with the family for twenty-four years, when she came direct from an orphanage as an under-maid on probation. Write about, or act out, some of the incidents when she has made mistakes in her job.

4 Write a record of a day in Arthur Winslow's life as a bank manager.

5 At the end of the play Catherine tells Sir John that she will see him in Parliament. *But not in the Gallery. Across the floor.* In other words she intends one day to be an MP herself. Write the report in *The Times* which gives an account of one of her debates with Sir Robert in the House of Commons.

6 Grace says that when he has grown up, Ronnie will not thank Arthur for fighting his case so publicly. How do you think Ronnie will feel about this ten years later? Write a letter which he might send to his parents as he recalls the events ten years on.

7 Do you think Catherine will marry Desmond? Write a series of letters between them in which Catherine gives her answer and Desmond his response to it.

8 Write a newspaper obituary for any one of the characters, which would sum up her or his character and her or his life and work.

9 What impression do you get of the oncoming 1914-18 war? How far do the characters understand its significance? Work in a small group to find out about the First World War and its effects on the ordinary person. You could start by answering the following questions:

- Who was signed up? What were conditions like at the front?
- What did women do during the war? What might they have liked and disliked about the work?
- What happened to children during the war? How was family life affected?
- What differences were there for servants?

10 Share your findings with one another and then each take on one of the characters to act in role. Imagine a family meal after the war where the whole family meet up for the first time. In role, hold a conversation in which the characters consider the events before and during the war. You could also have an observer or an audience who can assess how well each character has been portrayed.

Extending the scenes

On several occasions characters are interrupted in the middle of conversations so that we are only given a hint as to their true feelings. As well as this ambiguity, the plot itself might have been changed had the conversations been completed.

☐ Continue the dialogue in one of the following scenes:

- Act 1, scene 1. Grace and Catherine are looking out into the garden at a small figure hiding in the rain. They are trying to decide who it is when John arrives.

  GRACE *Why can't he stick to his own garden?*
- Act 1, scene 1. John and Catherine are talking about their relationship when Ronnie appears from the garden.

  JOHN *You might be a little more explicit...*

- Act 1, scene 1. John and Catherine are talking about how Arthur Winslow will react to Ronnie's expulsion when Desmond arrives.

  CATHERINE (simply) *It might kill him –*

- Act 1, scene 1. The family are about to make a toast to John and Catherine's engagement when Violet lets out the secret that Ronnie is home.

  ARTHUR *Ah, Violet! We mustn't leave you out. You must join in the toast.*

- Act 1, scene 2. Catherine and Sir Robert are talking about the trial of Len Rogers when Grace comes in.

  SIR ROBERT *So I understand.* (After a faint pause) *As it happens, however, he was guilty.*

- Act 2, scene 1. Arthur and Catherine are talking about Sir Robert when he arrives.

  CATHERINE *Oh, I agree. But don't fool yourself about him, Father, for all that. The man is a fish, a hard, cold-blooded, supercilious, sneering fish.*

- Act 2, scene 1. Sir Robert is asking Catherine about her work for women's suffrage when John arrives.

  SIR ROBERT (murmuring) *Dear me! What sacrifice you young ladies seem prepared to make for your convictions –*

- Act 2, scene 1. Catherine and John are discussing the implications of the trial on their marriage when the phone rings.

  JOHN *Well, then, that's all I want to know. Darling! I was sure nothing so stupid and trivial could possibly come between us.*

- Act 2, scene 2. Arthur and Catherine are talking about Sir Robert when Desmond appears.

  CATHERINE (indifferently) *There's nothing in him to like or dislike, Father. I admire him.*

- Act 2, scene 2. Arthur and Catherine are discussing whether Catherine will marry Desmond when their attention is taken by a newspaper boy shouting outside.

  CATHERINE (with a smile) *In the words of the Prime Minister, Father, wait and see.*

Do you think your extra scenes improve or spoil the play?

Why do you think Rattigan chose to cut these conversations short?

Reflections

The play does not give time for the characters to reflect deeply on the actions they have taken or the attitudes they hold. When people write their memoirs they look back on situations and are able to decide upon their reactions towards them.

☐ Write the memoirs of some of the characters, focusing on the events stated below. Remember that they will be written some years later.

- Dickie thinks about the time when he had to give up his life at Oxford and start work in a bank.
- Catherine considers her changing attitude towards Sir Robert Morton.
- Arthur reflects on his decision to fight for his son's innocence.
- Grace looks back on her own experience of the courtroom.
- Sir Robert Morton remembers his meetings with, and attitude towards, Catherine Winslow.
- Violet recalls the day that Ronnie returned home early.
- Miss Barnes remembers her interview with Arthur Winslow.
- Desmond relives the day he proposed to Catherine.
- John considers what other action he might have taken after his father sent Arthur Winslow a letter.
- Ronnie remembers his first meeting with Sir Robert Morton.
- John discusses the Winslow case with his father, his new wife and his father-in-law.
- Ronnie remembers being cross-examined in the courtroom.

Staging the play

A play is designed to be staged. Although reading and studying may help us to understand it better, we should not forget that it was created to be watched. The following assignments are intended to make you think about how the play might be produced.

1. The play is set just before the First World War (1914-18) in the drawing room of a middle-class home. The room is described in the stage directions preceding the first scene, and we are told of more details as the play progresses. Looking at these, and having carried out some research into the furniture and décor of the period, imagine a photograph of any one moment in the action. Draw the photograph, labelling objects and explaining their importance to the scene, for example, *A = the silver cigarette box on the table centre stage from which Catherine takes a cigarette.*

2. The clothes of the pre-war period differ greatly from modern fashions. Having carried out some research into the fashion of the period, design a wardrobe for any *two* characters in the play. Their clothes will alter from scene to scene, and in order to make your decisions, you will need to refer to stage instructions, words spoken by characters and the fashion of the period, as well as deciding what suits the temperament of each character. Explain each of your choices with reference to all the above points.

3. Rattigan has given full stage instructions as to the emotions and actions of his characters at any point in the play. Imagine you are the director of a television production of *The Winslow Boy* and complete the following tasks:

   - You can chose exactly what the camera, and thus the audience, will see in each scene. Watch a film or television drama taking note of the director's use of close-up shots, wide-angle scenes, and of all the choices he makes about what the audience sees. What is the effect of each kind of shot? Now choose one brief episode in *The Winslow Boy* and indicate how you would film it and why.

- You have the choice to film some of your scenes outside the Winslows' drawing room. Which scenes would you chose, where would they be, and why?
- You can choose to film some additional scenes in the play, of events which are mentioned but not seen (for example, the trial). Which scenes would you add and why?

4 Imagine you are a director whose cast is about to begin rehearsals for *The Winslow Boy*. At this stage the actors are not quite sure of when their characters appear and what their relationship is to the other characters in the play. You advise them to keep a log of their character's appearances and their impressions of her or him and her or his relationship to others. Write a log which would be useful to an actor playing the part of Arthur, Grace, Catherine or Sir Robert Morton.

5 Work in a small group to act out a short scene from the play. You should begin by reading the scene through at least once, allowing each person to give her or his impressions of the scene and the characters in it. This should be followed by discussing one another's views and ensuring that the characters and actions match each other. There needs to be a period of time in which lines are learned, followed by a speak-through of the scene.

The whole scene can then be rehearsed, and discussed constructively to see if there are any areas for improvement, and to build up the confidence of each actor. You could aim to produce a whole act as a class, with each group taking a small scene, or to have each scene produced by two different groups to see how the groups' interpretations differ.

6 Try to see a production, or watch a video of *The Winslow Boy* (you might choose the BBC *Theatre Night* production, 1989), paying particular attention to how it is produced. How does it differ from your understanding of the play? What do you like about it? Are the characters as you imagined them? What would you alter? Write a review of the production.

Extension assignments

Throughout the play Rattigan allows small comments to have wider meanings. The following assignments are intended to place some of these statements under scrutiny. Each of the assignments requires discussion and note-taking, and could lead to oral presentations or essays.

1 ARTHUR ...*We'll see which is right – my instinct or your reason, eh?*

These are Arthur Winslow's words from Act 1, scene 2. To what extent do you see Kate as ruled by reason and Arthur by instinct? Find as many examples as you can from the play, which support or refute this opinion.

2 In Act 1, scene 1, the family discuss the vicar's sermon in church and Grace comments *What's the use of being good if you're inaudible?* To what extent does the play show that one needs to be audible as well as good?

3 Grace says of her daughter in Act 1, scene 1, *I don't think you modern girls have the feelings our generation did. It's this New Woman attitude.*
- What do the female characters in the play tell us about the changing position of women in the years before the First World War?
- In what ways have the rights of women been increased?
- Are there any ways in which women and men are still treated unequally?
- In what ways have women and men had to behave differently in order to bring about equality?

4 There are several references to the 'cost' of the trial to the family, both financial and emotional. Which character in the play do you feel pays the greatest price for Ronnie's innocence? You will need to look at each character in turn and consider the sacrifices she or he has made.

Suggestions for further reading

The Collected Plays of Terence Rattigan appear in four volumes. Each of the first three volumes contains a Preface by the playwright himself. The fourth collection of plays is introduced by B A Young and looks at Rattigan's work as a whole as well as making particular reference to the later plays.

The plays of Rattigan which may provide particular interest in relation to *The Winslow Boy* are *The Browning Version* (1948), *The Deep Blue Sea* (1952) and *Separate Tables* (1954). Another of his plays which uses an actual trial as its basis is *Cause Célèbre* (1977). It was originally written for radio, is fast moving with short dramatic scenes, and provides an interesting comparison to *The Winslow Boy*.

Other plays considering similar themes, such as social injustice and the rights of the individual, which could be read alongside *The Winslow Boy* are:

An Inspector Calls   by J B Priestley

The Devil's Disciple   by George Bernard Shaw

The Caucasian Chalk Circle   by Bertolt Brecht

A Man For All Seasons   by Robert Bolt

Savages   by Christopher Hampton

Whose Life Is It Anyway?   by Brian Clark

The Merchant of Venice   by William Shakespeare

The following novels (N), stories (S) and poems (P) also consider similar aspects of human life:

Individual rights:

It's My Life   by Robert Leeson (N)

Roll of Thunder Hear My Cry   by Mildred D Taylor (N)

Pin Money   by Jennifer Gubb (S)

Hard Times   by Charles Dickens (N)

Love between rivals:

Pride and Prejudice   by Jane Austen (N)

The power of the individual:

First They Said   by Alice Walker (P)

Still I Rise   by Maya Angelou (P)

Nineteen Eighty-Four   by George Orwell (N)

Equality for women:

Sisters are doing it for themselves   by The Eurythmics (song)

Edith Jackson   by Rosa Guy (N)

War:

The Soldier   by Rupert Brooke (P)

This is No Case of Petty Right or Wrong   by Edward Thomas (P)

The law:

Law Like Love   by W H Auden (P)

Bleak House   by Charles Dickens (N)

Wider reading assignments

1. Read any other play by Terence Rattigan and discuss the ways in which the two plays are similar. In what ways can you tell they are written by the same writer?

2. Read any other of the plays listed above, by a playwright other than Rattigan. What similar themes are tackled in both plays? How do the playwrights approach the topics differently?

3. Read a book and/or poem from the list above, which considers a theme found in *The Winslow Boy*. Prepare a talk in which you explain the different ways in which the themes are tackled.

4. Read any of the prefaces written by Terence Rattigan to his collected plays. What new things have you learned about the writer and his attitude to writing?